"As a scholar in coach education, I constantly seek innovative approaches that serve all athletes. This book delivers precisely that. For too long, sport has clung to a narrow, hierarchical view of leadership. This insightful book dismantles those limitations, offering a powerful, inclusive alternative in 'coaction' and provides a compelling and actionable framework for coaches to move beyond traditional, exclusionary leadership models. Prepare to rethink how you empower your athletes – this book is a game-changer."

Nicole M. LaVoi, PhD, Director, *Tucker Center for Research on Girls & Women in Sport, University of Minnesota*

"Sport in our country is in desperate need of a revolution, and shifting from leadership to coaction is the way. This book invites us to shift our mindset and actions on and off the field to create a sports culture that is healthier and athletes who are empowered, interconnected, and more fully actualized. Dr. Line hits the perfect mix of theory and practice, highlighting the voices of athletes, coaches, and experts in the field. Rigorous and inspiring, deeply exciting and immediately accessible, this book will be a constant companion for coaches, administrators, athletes and parents. Dr. Line sees the future of sports clearly and shows how coaction will lead us all to more joy, transformation, and community in sport."

Ellie Roscher, *Author of* Fair Game: Trans Inclusion and the Future of Sports

"A must read for anyone who plays a role within a group or team, with a special focus on athletic coaches, administrators, and support staff involved in sports. Anyone who works with others will find value in these pages. In particular, those who view the world through a collective lens, appreciate the power of collaboration and recognize that a team's strength lies in its members' unique qualities will discover validation, visibility, and encouragement to trust their instincts, along with practical tools and strategies to immediately apply. This book is for those who know there has to be a better way."

Barb Anthony, MSSA LISW-S, *Founder/Executive Director of Play Gap*

Building Coactive Sport Teams

Building Coactive Sport Teams develops and presents an asset-focused framework to guide coaches in engaging athletes as coactors. This book provides an asset-focused, inclusive approach to involving all team members in collaborating to achieve shared goals, a process called coaction. It lays out a coaching model that cultivates athletes' collaboration skills and increases team members' engagement, especially among those with diverse identities, skills, and experiences in working toward shared goals.

Using storytelling and offering an interactive format, this book translates interdisciplinary scholarship into a practical step-by-step process coaches can immediately apply to their teams. Stories highlight coach and athlete coactors, providing rich insight to help readers account for power, identities, and social context while advancing team goals. Each chapter has reflection questions to guide readers in applying the ideas within their team context.

This book is key reading for coaches and students in sport management programs, college administrators, and anyone interested in leadership development and collaboration.

Jo Line, PhD, is the Program Director for Community-Engaged Research and Learning and a lecturer at Oberlin College, US who has spent over a decade studying sport from a socio-cultural perspective. They are the Athletics Inclusive Climate and Belonging Senior Specialist for the nonprofit Athlete Ally, consulting with college and university athletic departments nationwide to promote LGBTQIA+ inclusion in sport. They apply an intersectional approach to examine facilitators and barriers to athletes' participation in and enjoyment of sport, with the aim of encouraging inclusive and collaborative team cultures that enable every team member to thrive. Jo's expertise in engaging team members in coaction is informed by their personal experience navigating competitive and recreational sport environments around the world as a soft-spoken synergistic nonbinary queer white competitive distance runner, coaching NCAA Division I, NCAA Division III, USCAA, and post-collegiate competitive and recreational athletes, and their academic training in Exercise and Sport Studies and American Culture Studies. Jo is dedicated to helping coaches nurture athletes' individual and collective capacity by encouraging athletes to identify and apply their unique strengths while working toward team goals.

Building Coactive Sport Teams

From Leadership to Coaction

Jo Line

Routledge
Taylor & Francis Group
NEW YORK AND LONDON

First published 2026
by Routledge
605 Third Avenue, New York, NY 10158

and by Routledge
4 Park Square, Milton Park, Abingdon, Oxon, OX14 4RN

Routledge is an imprint of the Taylor & Francis Group, an informa business

For Product Safety Concerns and Information please contact our EU representative GPSR@taylorandfrancis.com. Taylor & Francis Verlag GmbH, Kaufingerstraße 24, 80331 München, Germany.

ISBN: 978-1-032-99692-9 (hbk)
ISBN: 978-1-032-99690-5 (pbk)
ISBN: 978-1-003-60548-5 (ebk)

DOI: 10.4324/9781003605485

Typeset in Times New Roman
by Newgen Publishing UK

For my OCXCTF teammates, running together is where this book took root.

Contents

Acknowledgments

I am grateful for the coactive coaches and athletes who share their stories and insights in this book. You inspire me and have made the process of envisioning what a coactive team does and can look like a joy.

I am grateful for the friends and colleagues who have offered feedback throughout the writing process. You have challenged me, stretched my perspective, helped me clarify ideas, and cheered me on.

I believe we are stronger together and I am certainly stronger due to the support of a deeply caring network of teammates, coaches, mentors, colleagues, and family.

Interviewee Biographies

All interviewees' self-ascribed identities are presented throughout the book according to what they shared when asked. I have highlighted what was salient to those with identities they chose to share. In the text below, I omitted commas between identities to emphasize their inseparability.

All coaches in the manuscript are current coaches who consented to be presented as themselves and to be interviewed as coactive coaches and to share their insights about leadership, collaboration, and athlete well-being. Their professional titles are listed below for context, and salient identities are shared in interview excerpts throughout this book.

All athletes were college athletes at the time of their interviews, which I conducted for my dissertation: "Challenging the leadership narrative in sport: An exploration of NCAA division I women student-athletes' understandings of leadership" ([Doctoral dissertation, Bowling Green State University]. OhioLINK Electronic Theses and Dissertations Center. http://rave.ohiolink.edu/etdc/view?acc_num=bgsu1626709771716249). A pseudonym is included with athletes' self-ascribed identities for confidentiality. I also include the sport athletes were currently playing and their year in school at the time of the interview to provide additional context.

Dawn Staley, Head Women's Basketball Coach at the University of South Carolina is also featured as a coactor coach throughout this book. I drew upon publicly available interviews for her quotes and my analysis of her approach.

Coaches

Danny Feldman: Head Men's & Women's XC Coach/Assistant Track & Field Coach (Distance) at Bates College

Kadine Johnson-Crowder: Associate Head Coach for Men's and Women's Track & Field at Chicago State (Men's and Women's Track & Field and Cross Country Head Coach at Penn State Harrisburg at the time of the interview)

KC Woodford: Co-Owner of Yoga Squared, Co-Owner of Akron Athletic Collective, Yoga Instructor, Personal Trainer

Nikki Shell: Co-Owner of Yoga Squared, Co-Owner of Akron Athletic Collective, Yoga Instructor

Athletes

Ana: Biracial woman fourth-year gymnastics student-athlete

Audra: White Filipino fourth-year gymnastics student-athlete

Bailey: White woman first-year track and field student-athlete

Cara: White Christian woman second-year basketball student-athlete

Erica: White Christian female fourth-year track and field student-athlete

Fiona: Female first-generation college student second-year track and field student-athlete

Jackie: African American fourth-year gymnastics student-athlete

Kai: Woman international student third-year basketball student-athlete

Kate: Christian girl first-year track and field student-athlete

Kenza: African American woman fourth-year basketball student-athlete

Kim: White Christian female American third-year track and field student-athlete

Lily: White Christian woman first-year track and field student-athlete

Maria: Christian woman first-year track and field student-athlete

Milana: Christian woman transfer student second-year track and field student-athlete

Mina: Mixed-race Christian second-year track and field student-athlete

Molly: White Christian girl third-year track and field student-athlete

Nicole: Christian woman third-year track and field student-athlete

Piper: White heterosexual female third-year basketball student-athlete

Sasha: African American Christian female third-year track and field student-athlete

Sonya: Second-year track and field student-athlete

Tori: White Christian heterosexual girl first-year track and field student-athlete

1 Why We Need to Think Differently about Athlete Leadership Development

"Why is no one stepping up to lead?"

I've heard many coaches ask this question when seeking team captains. But what if it's the wrong question? What if the way we think about leadership in sport is actually limiting our ability to support athletes' development as engaged team members? In this book, I flip the narrative from tired, deficit-based leadership development strategies to inclusive, asset-based strategies that facilitate collaboration and provide athletes with the skills they need to thrive in and beyond sport.

As you read, I invite you to reflect on an alternative question: how can I enable each team member to actively contribute their strengths to our team's work together?

In the following chapters, I offer strategies you can use to cultivate all your team members' skills and provide opportunities for them to contribute their strengths through co-developed, coordinated efforts. Depending upon a few team members to guide your team diminishes everyone else's strengths and limits their contributions. If you expect team members to *develop into* leaders, you might ask yourself why you view them as incapable of leading now. In what ways are they currently contributing to the team yet not receiving recognition?

I offer an alternative, collaborative approach to team members working together, termed "coaction" by Karen L. Suyemoto and Mary Ballou (2007). On a coactive team, all members are valuable, and their differences are celebrated. Every member has strengths. Every member has opportunities for growth. Coaction enables all team members to apply and enhance their individual strengths and integrate them into a dynamic and ongoing process to maximize their collective

DOI: 10.4324/9781003605485-1

capacity. These strengths extend beyond sport-specific technical and tactical skills.

Technical and tactical skills only go so far if athletes do not feel safe, are unable to focus, or do not work effectively together. For example, one outgoing, vivacious team member may help raise the team's energy before an intense workout while a reserved, highly considerate team member may be athletes' go-to person when they need to talk through a challenge in their life. Neither needs to change their inclinations to fill the other role; they complement one another and they both support the team in important ways.

Multiple athletes on teams I coached expressed doubts about their ability to lead and questioned their value to the teams. These conversations prompted me to start researching inclusive and collaborative approaches to leadership. I began asking athletes how they thought they should lead in informal conversations and my doctoral research; frequently, they described demonstrating compliance with their coaches' directions and enforcing rules among their teammates (Line, 2021). I argue throughout this book that if an athlete perceives leadership as compliance, they are not learning to lead. They are learning to follow. How can an athlete "step up" to lead when they are focused on carefully following their coach and making sure others do the same?

As I worked with fellow coaches to provide leadership education for athletes, I also grew increasingly concerned that the narratives in books about leadership focus on individuals *becoming* leaders, often through actions that exemplified independent effort and self-sacrifice. Yes, you read that correctly. This narrative aligns with long-standing, popular leadership models such as transformational leadership and servant leadership, which have been demonstrated to offer effective guidance for leading. "So, why were you concerned?" you may ask.

Counterintuitive though it may seem, leadership, even leadership intended to be inclusive and relationship-focused, is an exclusionary concept. If a coach does not identify an athlete as a leader, they are a follower—inferior by default. A hierarchy is inherent to leadership. Encouraging athletes to *lead* others creates an environment in which athletes must prove their superiority over others to be recognized as leaders, rather than encouraging them to *collaborate with* one another. Encouraging athletes to *become* leaders also diminishes the ways they already influence and support one another.

If you are invested in building a team that prioritizes working effectively with one another and provides opportunities for *all* athletes' holistic growth, consider the following scenarios and questions:

- While hierarchy is inherent to leadership, with the leader positioned in a superior role over followers, leaders are dependent on followers. For example, we know a basketball team can't win a game with just a point guard. The point guard guides team members, but a coordinated effort among players in different positions results in scoring points. Is an athlete who passed the ball less important than the athlete who received and shot the ball? All team sports require different positions. Although athletes who play individual sports do not have different positions, team members who share leadership responsibilities enhance their efforts. For example, cross country runners can run in a pack. A different runner in the pack could pace their teammates each mile, distributing the effort of setting the pace across all the runners. If every athlete plays an important role during competitions, why would we divide them into leaders and followers?
- If an athlete has not been in a formal leadership role previously, will they perceive themselves as capable of leading? Konoval and colleagues point out that "individuals who are consistently held in a specific rank could come to internalize their rank as a truth" (2019, p. 132).[1] In other words, if an athlete is never selected as a captain or told they have leadership abilities, they may perceive themselves as incapable of leading. They may accept the role of follower. Self-motivation develops through receiving support from other people. A key factor in developing intrinsic motivation is fulfilling our need to feel competent (Deci & Ryan, 1985). An athlete who has not been told they have leadership skills is unlikely to believe they can be a competent leader. Being told that you *should* lead does not indicate that you *can* lead. How do you demonstrate that all your athletes are valuable and capable contributors?
- If an athlete perceives themselves as capable of leading, have they been offered formal or informal guidance about how to do so? They may look to role models in positions of leadership, but being in a formal leadership position does not ensure effective leadership (Fransen et al., 2014). If an athlete seeks to prove themselves a capable leader, they may be hesitant to ask for assistance or admit that

they do not know what they need to do. Who does a leader look to for support if followers are inferior and not responsible for guiding the group? If a leader *leads* others, they must rise above, not work *with,* them. Athletes may believe they cannot show self-doubt or let anyone know if they make a mistake, or they risk being perceived as incapable. Within the context of a group or team, they may be told that they are experiencing imposter syndrome. The concept of imposter syndrome frames this fear as an individual problem by placing the burden of responsibility on the individual to "overcome" it. This ignores the reality that self-perception is shaped by interactions with others (Tulshyan & Burey, 2021). How do you demonstrate that each athlete is a valuable team member, just as they are? How do you communicate that you believe in their ability to continue growing?

- Research indicates that athletes perceive team members other than captains as leaders and that athletes regard shared leadership as more effective. According to Fransen et al. (2020), athletes (ranging from regional- to national-level teams) see their coaches as better leaders when leadership is distributed among team members. We know from the research that athletes step into different leadership roles (Fransen et al., 2014). Despite decades of research, there is no single set of behaviors or one consistent approach to leadership among athletic teams. The possibility that team members play multiple leadership roles and/or take turns leading explains why this may be true. If leadership is limited to one or a few people, and if we expect leaders to consistently lead the same way, what types of contributions might the team miss out on?
- Externally imposed leadership expectations don't ensure athletes' investment in them or foster effective leadership. If a coach sets expectations for athletes about how they should lead, athletes may or may not share them. This is distinct from the athletes not being interested; an athlete may feel that an expectation is exclusive or may not believe they can lead in the way the coach expects. Requiring compliance with imposed expectations risks alienating team members with strengths not labeled as "leadership." If athletes focus on complying, the resulting hostile environment can detract from their ability to connect and collaborate with others and enjoy playing their sport (Porges, 1995, 2022). Externally imposed expectations may also limit athletes' intrinsic motivation (Deci & Ryan, 1985; Heywood, 2011). Involving athletes in establishing expectations signals that their perspectives matter, and their insights

can help the team be welcoming and successful. Accounting for athletes' perspectives can enhance their sense of competence and autonomy, contributing to their intrinsic motivation (Deci & Ryan, 1985). How do you involve athletes in co-creating expectations for how your team members work together?

- Traditional leadership narratives and sport culture encourage self-sacrifice (Greenleaf, 1970; Hughes & Coakley, 1991). Coaches and athletes repeat the phrases "no pain, no gain" and "there is no 'I' in team." However, there is a distinct difference between the discomfort of physically or psychologically challenging oneself athletically and experiencing physical or psychological pain. Athletes expect to encounter challenges in sport. Indicating that a good athlete is willing to push themselves through pain encourages athletes to ignore crucial signs from their body that their well-being is at risk to earn others' respect. If there is no "I" in team, an athlete may fear being perceived as selfish for expressing their needs. If we want athletes to support one another, why would we tell them they should not care for themselves?
- Popular leadership narratives also minimize the harms athletes may have endured, which impacts their sports experience. Approximately two-thirds of adults in the United States endured at least one Adverse Childhood Experience (ACE), which may result in trauma (Swedo et al., 2023). Although anyone may have ACEs, people with minoritized social identities, including those based on race, ethnicity, gender, sexuality, or ability, must navigate systemic discrimination in their everyday lives (Vazquez-Newsum, 2023). Harm is not independent of sport—in fact, many harmful incidents occur within the context of sport. The U.S. Center for SafeSport conducted an Athlete Culture and Climate Survey in 2024, including 3,762 former athletes across 67 sports and varied competitive levels. Findings showed that "78.4% of athletes shared that they had experienced behaviors related to emotional harm and neglect during their sports involvement". (U.S. Center for SafeSport, 2024, p. 5) A sense of connection and belonging is fundamental to resilience (Schwartz, 2024). If we aim to support athletes' holistic growth, why would we encourage them to demonstrate they can lead by minimizing their experiences of harm?

Throughout this book, I guide you in imagining what effective collaboration on your team could look like if we put aside the traditional concept of leadership. I invite you to question why we prioritize developing leaders—and label only a few athletes with that privileged title—over helping every athlete become an effective coactor. In the chapters to come, we will consider how traditional leadership practices constrain athletes' opportunities to discover and develop their strengths and explore how we can transform these practices and enable athletes to own their power and grow as engaged coactors. Throughout the process of this imagining, I provide opportunities for you to reflect on your current coaching practices and how they relate to traditional approaches to teaching leadership, the cultivation of coactors, and steps you can take to further support athletes' holistic development.

I share stories of people in several sport and physical activity leadership roles who model coaction in their work. Traditional sport structures (e.g., the athletic director/coach/captain hierarchy) currently limit the full adoption of coaction in place of leadership, but these coactors demonstrate strategies for integrating coaction within existing structures. As you read about these strategies, I invite you to imagine how a complete shift from leadership to coaction might impact athletes' safety, well-being, and development as collaborative team members. Narratives about real athletes and coaches' experiences illustrate key aspects of coaction. These coactors have given me permission to share their stories. As noted in the interviewee biographies, I refer to some by their real names and others with pseudonyms. I hope these stories provide examples of coactors for your team and that you continue seeking similar stories from your colleagues and the athletes you coach.

As a high school and college athlete competing in women's cross country and track and field, finding stories about strong, successful women athletes celebrated for their athleticism, especially runners, was difficult. People consistently recommended books on men's experiences, such as *Running with the Buffalos* and *Born to Run*. In these books, the men simply got to be great athletes. The one book about a woman runner that was offered to me was *What Made Maddy Run*, a story focused on her mental health struggles, in which competitive running is a source of stress. As I discuss throughout this book, we need to recognize the complexity of athletes' experiences, which includes supporting their mental health. However, as a college athlete seeking stories that celebrate women's athleticism, I saw a void.[2] [3] When I became a coach, I continued my search for more diverse examples of sport leaders and began researching sport leadership as a doctoral student. In seeking stories of model coactors for my research and this book, I decided to change the narrative once again and sought stories of those with diverse identities and lived experiences. It has been evident throughout my search that resources for leadership development persistently privilege the perspectives of white men (Vazquez-Newsum, 2023).

Have you researched the authors of the books you have relied on for leadership development? What lens do they view leadership through? Whose experiences and insights may be outside this lens and, therefore, more likely to be overlooked or unaccounted for?

The consequences of envisioning and teaching about leadership from a limited standpoint are apparent in the college athletic community. Women consistently fill less than half of the head coaching positions for women's National Collegiate Athletic Association (NCAA) Division I athletic teams (Goorevich et al., 2025; Lapchick, 2022). They are nearly absent as head coaches of men's teams, holding just over 4.5% of head coaching positions for men's NCAA Division I athletic teams as of 2022 (Lapchick, 2022). Women are also underrepresented among Athletic Directors, making up only 25% of athletic directors across Division I, II, and III as of 2024 (National Collegiate Athletic Association, 2024). Women with multiple minoritized identities have substantially less representation. As of 2024, 5% of athletic directors and 5% of head coaches across all NCAA divisions were women of color. While the NCAA only tracks binary gender identities and a limited number of racial and ethnic identities, researchers have also highlighted a heteronormative culture within athletics that hinders LGBTQIA+ coaches from discussing their families (LaVoi & Glassford, 2021). College athletes are emerging professionals in leadership roles in sport and other professional fields. Working toward equitable representation in these roles requires us to listen to, uplift, and learn from the experiences of members of communities with minoritized identities.

Dr. Nicole LaVoi makes clear your responsibility as a coach in this capacity: "[I]ndividuals who are seen and known in the world of sport, like coaches, communicate who and what is relevant and valued (and who is not)" (2016, p. 3). Athletes who do not see examples of people in leadership roles with qualities, identities, or experiences they relate to may give up on pursuing those roles because they can't envision themselves in leadership positions. As a coach, you may not share all the same identities as your athletes or know all your athletes' identities. However, sharing exemplary stories about people with diverse identities provides opportunities for your athletes to learn about role models they relate to while also developing their knowledge about people who are different from themselves.

Coaction, as this book describes, opens the door to a more fluid and contextual alternative to traditional leader-follower dynamics in sport. As coactors, team members co-determine what the team needs in the current context, and athletes contribute their strengths to meet these needs. At times, some athletes step into roles in which they guide teammates, while others follow that guidance. Those roles do not remain stable across time and change in response to the team's changing needs.

Depending upon one or a few designated leaders may put team members at risk in several ways. If a leader harms a follower, who is responsible for addressing that harm? A follower *follows*; they do not confront or question. A second risk of depending upon leadership is that leaders can face challenges or have a constrained bandwidth to contribute to team efforts. Their reduced capacity to engage in leadership responsibilities creates a void that others may be unprepared to fill. It may be unclear who should fill them. However, on a coactive team, no one is locked into a static role as a leader or a follower. It is expected that the collaborative process will be dynamic, and team members are prepared to adapt to support one another and the team.

I have had the opportunity to work with and observe many coaches who are invested in empowering athletes and are supportive and caring. Yet, their athletes did not readily ask questions or share their perspectives. Inviting athletes to contribute their perspectives is integral to cultivating a collaborative team environment. However, this relationship-oriented action must be preceded by building a team environment where athletes feel safe expressing their honest perspectives without fear of repercussions.

Leaders may also intend to support their followers, but their actions may not achieve their intended outcome (Denison et al., 2017). For example, a college coach may believe they provide helpful guidelines during a track interval workout by telling a runner to run 800-meter intervals in a specific time, six times in a row. A runner who did not sleep the night before because they were studying for an exam might perceive this workout as stressful and increasing their physical fatigue rather than improving their fitness. However, if they're worried about appearing committed to their training, they may not ask the coach if they can adjust their workout to support their holistic well-being. In an environment that supports athletes in speaking up, the runner and their coach can discuss the workout beforehand and decide what would be most beneficial to the runner's well-being that day.

Providing opportunities for all team members to think for themselves is often more effective for achieving team goals than requiring team members to passively follow the coach's instructions. Enabling all team members to use their inherent power means coaches must reflect on their practices and consider how they contribute to both the intended and unintended outcomes their team achieves (Denison et al., 2017). Sharing power is different from leadership and inherent to engaging in coaction, which can improve team members' ability to work together (Fransen et al., 2014).

My understanding of leadership changed in my third year of college coaching. I was an NCAA program's Assistant Cross Country and Track and Field Coach. I worked with two head coaches: Coach Carla Coffey, who oversaw track and field, and Coach Ellen O'Neil, who oversaw cross country. For the first time in my experience as an athlete and a coach, I worked with two women head coaches. During the indoor and outdoor track and field seasons, I worked alongside two other assistant coaches, Coach Dean Dumas and Coach Lara-Jane Que. We all came from different backgrounds and had varied gender, racial, ethnic, and sexual identities. Our personalities were as dissimilar as the events we coached. However, we learned from each other's unique perspectives and balanced one another through our contrasting personalities, enabling us to work with the team more effectively. Our unique ways of thinking helped us distribute tasks, maximizing our strengths while supporting each other's skill development.

Our coaching relationships grew as we encouraged each other at practices, asked for input, shared our experiences, and laughed together. Our commitment to supporting one another was clear to the team as the seasons progressed. Athletes from different event groups chatted during our warm-up, which we intentionally designed to include all event groups, and cheered for each other throughout practice and meets. We also encouraged collaboration through our athlete leadership structure. We created a rotating "weekly leader" role, taken on by two to three members at a time. This structure allowed athletes to take turns assuming responsibilities often expected of captains. Athletes who would typically shy away from a formal leadership role practiced skills for supporting and guiding team members alongside team members who were more comfortable with those activities. We were not separate event groups led by individual, specialized coaches; we were one collaborative team.

This experience eventually led me to research leadership development to better understand how college athletes define, practice, and learn about leadership. The following composite dialogue among college athletes resulted from a study I conducted with several women's teams to examine how college athletes define and learn about leadership. I share quotations from these athletes to highlight limitations of the traditional conceptualization of leadership on sport teams.[4]

Audra: Leading by example is something that I really take to heart because I'm not as great at confrontation or speaking up as well as other people might be, but I think I'm really good at taking what's supposed to be done and showing that to other people.

Maria: Me too. I'm not gonna be super vocal, but I always do what I'm asked.

Sasha: Something that differentiates between being a leader and not being a leader is submitting yourself to authority, no matter what position you are in. I think that's a really big thing, when you're at that point where you can submit yourself to authority. You may not like that you have to write a ten-page paper, but you're gonna do it because it's gonna get you the grade, it's going to take you further. You may even learn something along the way.

Tori: I agree. For example, if someone were to say, "Go back and do two hundred abs," I want to make sure I do all two hundred abs and not cut it short. That's one of my main ones, just doing what's asked of me, and if I don't do that, then that kind of hurts me inside. I feel kind of guilty when I don't do that, so that's why it's such a big part of me, just the feeling I get when I don't get something accomplished.

Fiona: I take instructions. I'm not really a verbal leader, but I can lead by example.

Sonya: "Doing the right thing" is on the path to leadership… because you have to be a good influencer; you can never be a bad influencer. You have to always do what's right even though it may not be the popular opinion.

Kim: I think it is important to be able to point out mistakes when they are made. I'm pretty good at that. I know what I should be doing and what I shouldn't be doing, and if somebody's not doing the right thing, then I know it.

Nicole: When I was a captain in high school, my coach made me be a leader by example so that people would do the same thing I would do. I felt like I was a leader in high school, but I feel like I was more of a friend that excelled so other people did the same thing as me. I didn't feel like a boss, I didn't boss anybody around, I didn't tell anybody what to do, I was kind of just like, "This is what I'm gonna do; if you want to do it, then do it, if you don't then don't." Also, if what I'm doing isn't the right way, I learn from other people the right way to do something that I can show other people how to do it.

What do you observe from this dialogue? Do these athletes sound like self-assured, self-directed leaders?

I found this dialogue troubling because athletes consistently described being an athlete leader in terms of compliance, following their coaches' rules, and modeling their coaches' expectations for other athletes. This understanding of leadership discourages athletes from thinking for themselves, offering their ideas and insights, and speaking out against harm. Rather than becoming successful leaders in and beyond sport, these athletes are learning to be good followers, even in supposed leadership positions. How can an athlete identify their strengths or discover and develop new ones if conforming to external expectations is the path to recognition? Furthermore, if we only celebrate those who conform to imposed expectations, we miss the opportunity to learn about athletes' unique assets and discourage individual expression.

Some athletes discussed aiming to lead by example. Leading by example is dependent upon knowing what ideal leadership is for the present context and those around you. How can you know what others need if you prioritize your own vision of what a leader should be? Furthermore, if team members are expected to follow your example without additional guidance, this creates an idealized conformity. The following dialogue highlights several athletes' perspectives on leading by example:

Lily: I'm more of a lead-by-example type person until I am fully comfortable and feel like it is my place to say something.

Kai: Yeah, I am comfortable with leading others by actions.

Tori: I was a little more vocal back in high school when I moved up through seniority. As a senior, obviously, you can be more vocal. I act in a way a successful athlete would act, and I expect my teammates to act that way, too. Leading by example is a little bit easier as a freshman, even though sometimes people aren't gonna look at the freshmen as, "Oh, let me do it because she's doing it," cuz seniority. I'm hoping next year, once the new class comes in that, like, they can see that in me and then also kind of go along.

Milana: I do, too. I just kinda do what I expect other people to do, and I hope that they see that and do the same thing, which isn't always the case. I'm most comfortable leading with my team by promoting the best thing to do at practice, even if it's not the easiest, and encouraging my teammates to communicate and take care of themselves by intentionally doing that in my life.

Kate: I'm most comfortable leading in positions where I can demonstrate my drive and work ethic.

Erica: I think I mostly lead by example. I always try to be positive and encouraging. I try not to overpower people and control them. People look up to me because of the way I carry myself, I think.

Several athletes described opting to lead by example rather than vocally because it feels comfortable. Of course it does: if you lead in a way that matches your vision, you avoid overt conflict. Alternatively, engaging in dialogue with your team to collaboratively develop a shared set of expectations for engaging in coaction means conflict is sure to arise. What many athletes don't realize is that this is a good thing.

To lead by example, a person must know what ideal leadership is. However, one athlete's opinions about a leader's ideal actions may not support their team members' needs. A lack of vocal dissent does not mean dissent does not exist. It means no one on the team feels comfortable expressing it. If a team has cultivated a welcoming, supportive, collaborative culture, conflicts open the door to practicing effective communication, learning more about one another, and expanding team members' perspectives.

It's time to change the leadership narrative to better serve all athletes and participants in sport. Coaction is an approach to effective collaboration that maximizes the involvement of all team members and encourages their continuous development as engaged collaborators, or coactors.[5]

In addition to encouraging team members to collaborate, value diverse strengths, and attend to one another's unique needs, coaction also requires team members to be attentive to power. This awareness includes understanding power dynamics between and among team members and how the team structure influences them. If coaches, other team staff members, and athletes pay attention to power dynamics, they can identify, discuss, and break down barriers that limit opportunities for coaction.

Engaging in coaction means team members can practice hands-on learning about many possible ways of contributing to a team's collective goals, how to work with others with different strengths, support others' growth, and consider and effectively integrate diverse perspectives into collaborative strategies. As they engage in coaction, every team member gains the opportunity to identify their strengths and areas for growth, experience validation from coaches and teammates, and challenge themselves to enhance and expand their skills. The next chapter provides the research-based framework to guide your cultivation of a coactive team. The remaining chapters walk you through implementing this collaborative approach to working with your team.

Notes

1 This idea is informed by Michel Foucault's work, *Discipline and Punish: The Birth of the Prison.*

2 In 2022 and 2023, there was a surge in books by and about accomplished women runners, including Alison Mariella Désir, Lauren Fleshman, Kara Goucher, and Des Linden. Deena Kastor also released a book in 2018 and Goucher authored multiple training-oriented books beginning in 2011. While these books did showcase their athleticism, Désir, Fleshman, and Goucher also bore the burden of shedding light on systemic discrimination and abuse they have navigated throughout their athletic careers.

3 At the time, I was not aware of any elite nonbinary runners. This changed in 2023, when I saw transgender and nonbinary track and field athlete Nikki

Hiltz win the USA Track and Field National Championship and compete at the World Athletics Championships.

4 The quotations I present consist of participants' words. I arranged quotations from individual interviews that demonstrated the same theme into composite dialogues (cf. Krane et al., 2014) to highlight connections among different participants' ideas. Athlete dialogues throughout this book are composite dialogues.

5 As my co-authors and I explained in Line et al. (2025), "This model arose as a feminist approach to engaging in leadership, but we view this model as distinct from leadership due to the rejection of the leadership hierarchy and emphasis on equity" (p. 265).

References

Deci, E. L., & Ryan, R. M. (1985) *Intrinsic motivation and self-determination in human behavior*. Plenum Press.

Denison, J., Mills, J. P., & Konoval, T. (2017). Sports' disciplinary legacy and the challenge of 'coaching differently'. *Sport, Education and Society, 22*(6), 772–783. https://doi.org/10.1080/13573322.2015.1061986

Fransen, K., Mertens, N., Cotterill, S. T., Vande Broek, G., & Boen, F. (2020). From autocracy to empowerment: Teams with shared leadership perceive their coaches to be better leaders. *Journal of Applied Sport Psychology, 32*(1), 5–27. https://doi.org/10.1080/10413200.2019.1617370

Fransen, K., Vanbeselaere, N., De Cuyper, B., Vande Broek, G., & Boen, F. (2014). The myth of the team captain as principal leader: Extending the athlete leadership classification within sport teams. *Journal of Sports Sciences, 32*(14), 1389–1397. https://doi.org/10.1080/02640414.2014.891291

Goorevich, A., Czinano, M., Gordon, A., Martin, S., Overberg, E., Stevenson, B., & LaVoi, N. M. (2025). *Women in College Coaching Report Card: NCAA Division-I Select Institutions, 2024–25*. The Tucker Center for Research on Girls & Women in Sport.

Greenleaf, R. K. (1970). *The servant as leader*. Robert K. Greenleaf Publishing Center.

Heywood L. L. (2011). Affective infrastructures: Toward a cultural neuropsychology of sport. *Frontiers in Evolutionary Neuroscience, 3*(4), 1–5. https://doi.org/10.3389%2Ffnevo.2011.00004

Hughes, R. & Coakley, J. (1991). Positive deviance among athletes: The implications of over conformity to the sports ethic. *Sociology of Sport Journal, 8*(4), 307–325. http://dx.doi.org/10.1123/ssj.8.4.307

Konoval, T., Denison, J., & Mills, J. (2019). The cyclical relationship between physiology and discipline: One endurance running coach's experiences problematizing disciplinary practices. *Sports Coaching Review, 8*(2), 124–148. https://doi.org/10.1080/21640629.2018.1487632

Krane, V., Ross, S., Barak, K. S., Lucas-Carr, C. B., & Robinson, C. L. (2014). Being a girl athlete. *Qualitative Research in Sport, Exercise and Health*, *6*(1), 77–97. https://doi.org/10.1080/2159676X.2013.809380

Lapchick, R. E. (2022). *The 2022 race and gender report card: College sport.* Institute for Diversity and Ethics in Sport. www.tidesport.org/_files/ugd/c01324_d0d17cf9f4c7469fbe410704a056db35.pdf

LaVoi, N. M. (2016). Introduction. In N.M. LaVoi (Ed.), *Women in sports coaching* (pp. 1–9). Routledge.

LaVoi, N. M., & Glassford, S. L. (2021): "This is our family": LGBTQ family narratives in online NCAA D-I coaching biographies. *Journal of Homosexuality*, 1–24. https://doi.org/10.1080/00918369.2021.1921506

Line, J. (2021). *Challenging the leadership narrative in sport: An exploration of NCAA Division I women student-athletes' understandings of leadership* [Doctoral dissertation, Bowling Green State University]. OhioLINK Electronic Theses and Dissertations Center. http://rave.ohiolink.edu/etdc/view?acc_num=bgsu1626709771716249

Line, J., Kochanek, J., & Baeth, A. (2025). We do not need leaders. We need coactors. In V. Krane & T. Prewitt-White (Eds.), *Reimagining the gendering of sport.* Elgar Press.

National Collegiate Athletic Association. (2024). *NCAA demographics database* [Data visualization dashboard]. NCAA. www.ncaa.org/about/resources/research/ncaa-demographics-database

Porges, S. W. (1995). Orienting in a defensive world: Mammalian modifications of our evolutionary heritage. A Polyvagal Theory. *Psychophysiology, 32*(4), 301–18. https://doi.org/10.1111/j.1469-8986.1995.tb01213.x

Porges S. W. (2022). Polyvagal Theory: A science of safety. *Frontiers in Integrative Neuroscience, 16*, 1–15. https://doi.org/10.3389/fnint.2022.871227

Schwartz, A. (2024). *Applied Polyvagal Theory in yoga: Therapeutic practices for emotional health.* W. W. Norton.

Suyemoto, K. L., & Ballou, M. B. (2007). Conducted monotones to coacted harmonies: A feminist (re)conceptualization of leadership addressing race, class, and gender. In J. L. Chin, B. Lott, J. K. Rice, & J. Sanchez-Hucles (Eds.), *Women and leadership: Transforming visions and diverse voices* (pp. 35–54). Blackwell Publishing.

Swedo, E. A., Aslam, M.V., Dahlberg, L.L., Holditch Niolon, P., Guinn, A. S., Simon, T. R., & Mercy, J. A. (2023). Prevalence of Adverse Childhood Experiences among U.S. adults — Behavioral risk factor surveillance system, 2011–2020. *Morbidity and Mortality Weekly Report*, *72*, 707–715. http://dx.doi.org/10.15585/mmwr.mm7226a2.

Tulshyan, R., & Burey, J-A. (2021, February 11). *Stop telling women they have imposter syndrome.* Harvard Business Review. https://hbr.org/2021/02/stop-telling-women-they-have-imposter-syndrome

U.S. Center For SafeSport. (2024). *2024 Athlete culture & climate survey report.* https://uscenterforsafesport.org/wp-content/uploads/2024/07/CultureClimateSurvey_ExternalReport_071824_v1.6.pdf

Vazquez Newsum, J. (2023). *Untapped leadership: Harnessing the power of underrepresented leaders*. Globe Pequot.

2 The New Framework

The Coactive Process

As discussed in Chapter 1, hierarchy is inherent to leadership. This also means that leadership is a relational concept; a person must have followers to be a leader. The difference between a leader and their followers is positional authority; the leader's position grants them the authority to direct others (Batliwala, 2011). Others may look to a leader as an example, enabling them to influence behavior. If followers are inspired by the leader or feel obligated to comply with their directions, the leader shapes them.

This leader/follower division raises several questions for athlete leadership development:

- If a coach strives to empower athletes to develop as leaders, at what point does an athlete switch from a follower to a leader?
- What does "empowerment" mean if we view athletes as individuals who already have agency?
- If athlete leaders lead *alongside* their coach, who is in a leadership role with authority over them, how might athletes have to negotiate practicing leadership skills while following the coach?
- Can followers lead one another, or can only the coach and captain lead the team?

One day, when I was coaching cross country and track and field athlete Valerie[1], she expressed disappointment that she had not been appointed team captain. She wanted to be a team leader but felt she wouldn't have the opportunity to lead without that title.

"How might you contribute to the team without being a captain?", I asked her.

DOI: 10.4324/9781003605485-2

As we talked, she mentioned understanding that she could still impact her teammates without the title of captain but shared that the lack of formal recognition made her feel undervalued. I wondered how this discouragement might impact her enjoyment on the team and whether feeling her contributions were insignificant would reduce her motivation to continue developing as a leader. I had observed her impact on her teammates and had no doubt she influenced them in positive, important ways (Line, 2021).

A survey conducted by EY and espnW indicated that sport participation strongly correlates with leadership in professional careers outside of sport. Although women are underrepresented in the C-suite, among survey respondents, "94% of women in the C-suite played sport, 52% at a university level" (EY & espnW, 2015, p. 9). This may lead us to believe that sport provides the opportunity to develop skills that contribute to professional success. However, if an athlete does not feel supported as a developing leader, what opportunities to enhance these skills might they miss out on? What valuable skills might they possess that they do not get the opportunity to contribute because they have not been recognized as "leadership" skills? What future opportunities might they bypass due to a lack of belief in their ability to lead?

Valerie's concerns echoed my own experiences. Throughout my childhood and young adult years, I observed my louder, more outgoing peers get appointed to leadership roles on sport teams and in musical theater. Coaches and work supervisors told me I needed to be louder, more commanding, and more outgoing to lead. I recognized the importance of stretching myself to grow, but these expectations conflicted with my personality. As Susan Cain states in *Quiet*, "We like to think that we value individuality, but all too often we admire one *type* of individual—the kind who's comfortable 'putting himself out there'" (2013, p. 4). I was inclined to be an observer and preferred one-on-one or small-group interactions over speaking in front of a large audience. As an athlete, I didn't respond well to loud, commanding leadership, and I wondered, "Is that really always the ideal way to lead?" If it was, I wasn't sure I could or would even want to lead.

My college cross country and track and field coach, Coach Ray Appenheimer, taught me that I could be my soft-spoken, contemplative, collaborative self *and* be an impactful team member. His actions motivated me and helped me develop confidence as a valuable and influential team member. He has been a quiet yet persuasive and consistent presence in my life. Coach Appenheimer began recruiting me to join his college team in the fall of my junior year of high school via monthly phone calls. During these calls, he expressed genuine interest in getting to know me as a whole person, not just as an athlete who would compete for his team.

When I met him in person, I was struck by his unwavering eye contact, which I understood as an indication of his focused attention. Working with him is a two-way street. He shares his own experiences to demonstrate his understanding and to provide motivation. I trust him because he has shared his challenges and successes. This trust gave me confidence in the advice he provided. He expresses disappointment bluntly; there is no sugar-coating. However, it is in a one-on-one, thoughtful conversation, not a loud or public expression of anger. It is also short-lived and based on the event, not the person. Coach Appenheimer always believed in me more than I believed in myself, but he never told me what to do. Instead, he helped guide me toward success and left me to discover what I was capable of if I was willing to put the work in and trust the training process. He was interested in getting to know each individual person, what makes them tick, and meeting them where they were to help them grow.

The relationship-oriented actions that Coach Appenheimer modeled for my teammates and me encouraged us to build strong relationships with one another. The sense of support and belonging that I experienced on my team motivated me to give my best effort every day—in training and competitions. I viewed excelling in racing as a way of expressing my gratitude for my coach and my pride in being a part of that team. This contributed to my competitive success, earning NCAA All-American honors seven times as a collegiate cross-country and track and field athlete. I view this success as my team's collective success because I do not believe I would have had the same success without them.

Research backs me up. Our social environment shapes athletic performance in several ways, including how it impacts our nervous system (Heywood, 2011; Porges, 1995) and our motivation (Deci & Ryan, 1985). Traditional leadership tends to focus on the leader as an influential individual (Batliwala, 2011),[2] but there are alternative ways of thinking about effective collaboration that account for context and emphasize mutual influence among team members. As Batliwala (2011) explained,

> We often think of leaders in the traditional sense: a handful of people with high-ranking positions who have claimed the most power within their organization. Power is not shared in these structures because being successful means always competing to be "number one."
>
> (p. 33)

The *coactive process* framework presented in this chapter offers an alternative way to collaborate effectively and treats power-sharing as integral. The coactive process synthesizes and offers a guide for applying commonly overlooked ideas developed through research across several academic fields and work dedicated to promoting equity. These concepts and theories include the Feminist Leadership Diamond, coaction, the four ways a person can express their power, intersectionality, Self-Determination Theory, and Polyvagal Theory.

As we work to understand interpersonal dynamics and collaboration among diverse team members, insights from applied work in conjunction with research from law, psychology, and sociology offer valuable guidance. The concepts I include in this framework were not initially connected to sport, but they promote effective collaboration among teams[3] working to achieve shared goals. Regardless of which specific social issue the change-makers who authored these concepts addressed, they all offer valuable insights about relationship-building and power-sharing that enable coaches to model and teach inclusive practices for effective collaboration. Doing so means all team members, whether or not they hold formal leadership roles, can actively work together to achieve mutual goals. Throughout the following chapters, you will hear from real coactors in the sport and fitness industry who discuss the coactive strategies they employ with their own teams, why they have chosen these strategies, and how they have been impactful.

The shift from developing leaders to developing coactive teams can be difficult within the traditionally hierarchical and patriarchal (Evans & Pfister, 2021) sport culture. However, you and your team members get to decide what culture *you* want on *your* team. Over time, shifts in team cultures can lead to a more inclusive and collaborative culture in sport.

In this chapter, I provide an overview of the components of the coactive process. This overview lays the foundation for exploring how you can work with your team members to develop a coactive team.

The Feminist Leadership Diamond

Although it is clear that leadership is highly valued in sport and American society, what makes a person a leader or how a person should engage in leadership is less clear (Batliwala, 2011). Many leadership models exist, and there is no evidence that any specific model of leadership is ideal in all contexts. Common models for sport leadership include transformational (Bass, 1985; Burns, 1978; Downton, 1973) and servant leadership (Greenleaf, 1970).

Srilatha Batliwala's (2011) Feminist Leadership Diamond differs in that it does not prescribe specific leadership characteristics, actions, or behaviors. Instead, this model outlines how team members establish leadership expectations. Batliwala proposed that an organization could establish leadership practices aligned with feminist values such as equality, equity, inclusion, and human rights for all people. This model offers a guide for how a team could adopt a collaborative, equity-focused approach to leadership.

However, as long as we operate within the overarching framework of traditional leadership, our ability to share power equitably among team members and engage in truly collaborative practices is constrained by the leader-follower hierarchy. Batliwala and fellow change-makers' ideas can help us imagine shifting from investment in hierarchical leadership to coaction. If our goal is to equitably support the growth of every unique athlete on our team, we must go beyond inclusive and collaborative leadership. Coaction offers us language and a structure to imagine a way of truly working *together*.

The Feminist Leadership Diamond highlights that creating "ideal" and "normal" group interactions is a process influenced by many factors. Leadership and ideal actions and behaviors depend on context and community expectations. The Feminist Leadership Diamond model comprises five components: the self, power, principles and values, policies and purpose, and practices. Four of these—power, principles and values, policies and purpose, and practice—make up the diamond's quadrants and represent the process that informs ideals of "leadership." This process is embedded within the self, represented by a circle around the diamond. You can view the model in several ways, each supporting an exploration of how athletes learn and apply leadership. The first is viewing the process of defining leadership as occurring within each person; every single person has the capacity to be a leader. They view themselves as capable of enacting their version of leadership. Others around them must also perceive them as a leader, so this process does not occur in isolation—it is always contextual. Furthermore, a person's understanding of what leadership means and looks like is uniquely shaped by who they are. Their personal understanding of leadership informs how they engage in leadership.

Viewing Batliwala's model from another angle enables us to recognize other influences on leadership. If we consider the leadership diamond as an organization (such as a sport team), we can see the "self" circle as symbolizing each member bringing themselves to the organization. From this perspective, we can consider how team members are encouraged, enabled, discouraged, or prohibited from expressing their whole selves within the organization. This expression includes sharing their understanding of leadership: when team members join the team, are they told how they should look and behave if they want to be seen as a leader, or are team members invited to define what leadership consists of? Athletes are often taught that they should be leaders, but we do not always teach them what to do to become one.

On sport teams, athlete leaders are typically recognized with the title of Captain. Captains are expected to model proper leadership for the other athletes. However, reliance on formal athlete leaders modeling leadership encourages conformity; the other athletes learn that the way to be recognized as a leader is to act like those in leadership positions. If this becomes the norm, athletes who most easily conform and are most comfortable modeling themselves after current captains will be recognized as leaders. Meanwhile, athletes whose characteristics differ—identities, personalities, inclinations, or skills—will not receive the same recognition. The team will miss the opportunity to benefit from their contributions, and these team members are less likely to assert themselves and apply strengths that the team doesn't seem to value.

Engaging in the leadership process outlined in Batliwala's Feminist Leadership Diamond and emphasizing power-sharing can discourage conformity from becoming the norm. Instead, sharing power encourages team members to develop a strengths-focused mentality in which different contributions are valued as team members collaborate. However, engaging in leadership does not ensure that leaders are committed to collaboration or stay attentive to how power operates.

With this in mind, the coactive process includes components of Batliwala's leadership model but takes a different form. In the coactive process, collaboration and equity are the foundation, and interpersonal and structural power dynamics are integral to all interactions among team members.

The Coactive Process

Instead of a diamond, I represent the coactive process with a braid of ropes. Every member of the organization is a thread in each rope. Each member's presence, perspective, strengths, and areas for growth are all valuable to other members of the organization. We are social beings; we depend on others to live and thrive. A diverse set of perspectives allows us to examine a task or situation from different angles and facilitates innovation. Various strengths enable team members to contribute to a task uniquely, enabling creative and equitable collaborative efforts. Team members' areas for growth allow others to contribute their different strengths (Doyle, 2023). Like a braided rope, we are all stronger together.

The threads, or all of the unique team members, comprise the ropes that enable the organization to exist and operate; the way these threads come together is not a given. In the coactive process, four ropes form a braid. These ropes represent power, principles and values, politics and purpose, and practices. Each of these ropes is interdependent; just as the rope is stronger with all of the threads; the braid is stronger with each of the ropes.

The Self

When a person arrives anywhere, such as at a team practice, they show up as their entire self. Many things make up the self, including one's "particular attributes, talents, histories, experiences, and psychic structure" (Batliwala, 2011, p. 56). A person cannot put any of these aspects of themselves aside. Instead, they may choose which aspects of themselves to share. They may receive opportunities to share or face barriers to sharing certain parts of themselves. Research focused on sexually and gender-diverse people indicates that if an athlete consistently expects to be discriminated against due to aspects of who they are, this may negatively impact their well-being (Diamond & Alley, 2022). Differently, feeling comfortable expressing oneself authentically is associated with life satisfaction (Fletcher & Marvell, 2023). One study indicated that people who are encouraged to express themselves authentically during an interview receive higher performance evaluations (Gino et al., 2020).

If we apply these ideas to a sport team, we can see that an athlete's engagement with the team is not simply a matter of personal choice or self-motivation. If athletes with minoritized identities do not feel fully supported, they may hesitate to engage for the sake of self-protection. An athlete's sense of social safety may be thwarted if they are uncertain about receiving support for their whole self (e.g., disclosing invisible identities such as that they are bisexual or have attention-deficit/hyperactivity disorder (ADHD). Explicitly supportive actions can contribute to an athlete's sense of social safety (Diamond & Alley, 2022). Therefore, telling athletes to be actively engaged is unlikely to result in all team members' self-motivated engagement. Team members must actively demonstrate to one another that they value and support one another.

On a sport team, coaches and teammates may invite and encourage athletes to share their thoughts and contribute their strengths to team efforts. Alternatively, team members may be prohibited (intentionally or unintentionally) from openly expressing themselves.[4] The team's social environment and interactions with staff and teammates influence their ability to share. Consequently, the coach must intentionally cultivate a supportive and inclusive environment to enable athletes to express their whole selves on the team.

Power

Within the leadership hierarchy, we assume the person at the top possesses the most power. However, every person has power. They can think for themselves, generate new ideas, ask questions, and make decisions. This is called their power within (VeneKlasen & Miller, 2002). The difference between leaders' and their followers' power is the ability to express power and the resistance they face when they do. Within a hierarchical organization, people's ability to use their power increases as others defer to their authority (Batliwala, 2011). Due to their position, they may also possess responsibilities that allow them to exercise power, like making decisions that impact everyone in the organization (Batliwala, 2019).

Within American society, we often think of power as authority or force wielded over others. This understanding of power may lead someone to try to distance themselves from power. Some athletes tell me they do not want to be in a formal leadership position because they do not want to direct or control others. However, power is not inherently good or bad. Instead, a person's use of their power can positively or negatively impact others. Furthermore, power is not simply acquired and held. Power exists within each of us, interpersonally, and structurally.

Batliwala explains that power is

> impossible for anyone to capture or take away. 'Empowerment' is the process through which we try to get in touch with this essential power that we all carry within us. When we connect this inner power with the power that lies within others, we can build change processes that can dismantle and transform seemingly unchangeable power structures!
>
> (2019, p. 10)

Possessing power within does not mean every person can express their power to (VeneKlasen & Miller, 2002), or their ability to transform their power within into action. A person's ability to share their ideas, voice questions, make autonomous decisions, or contribute to collective decisions depends on their recognition of their own power, the opportunities they are given to exercise their power, and the constraints or barriers they face to doing so.

People express power to in two ways. The first is enacting power over others (VeneKlasen & Miller, 2002). This means they prioritize their ideas and expectations over others' ideas or expectations. They insist their ideas are correct and expect others to follow their directions and conform to their guidelines.

Alternatively, they may exercise their power with others (VeneKlasen & Miller, 2002). Power with is a form of collaboration. A person who expresses power with others invites them to share their ideas and feedback. They co-create strategies, goals, and plans. This does not mean they do not assert ideas, but rather that they do not insist their ideas are correct at the expense of other input. A team may choose to use one member's ideas in some circumstances and prioritize other team members' ideas at a different time or integrate several different ideas from multiple team members.

The four expressions of power show us that power is not inherently good or bad. Rather, how power is expressed leads to positive or negative outcomes, and a person's ability to use power can involve forcing others to comply or engaging in relationship-building that cultivates mutual investment. A coach can intentionally express their power with athletes and encourage them to do so with one another, assuming this encouragement is not manipulative or used as a means to a self-serving end. This mode of engagement contributes to relationships in which team members encourage one another to express their power.

Chapter 4, "Share the Power," provides practical recommendations for how coaches can express power with athletes and encourage athletes to express power with one another.

Principles and Values

On a team, principles and values provide the opportunity to express our needs and learn how to support others. While teams and organizations often have a shared set of values (Taylor, 2016), teams and organizations are made up of unique individuals. Every individual has principles and values. These do not change based on context. So, someone may join a team with whom they share interests, goals, and perhaps values and principles. However, declaring a set of top values for every member to demonstrate does not magically align everyone on the team.

Within the context of collegiate sport, numerous factors inform a person's decision to attend a college and join a team. The team's declared values may help them differentiate among the teams they are considering, but we cannot assume these values are the determining factor. An athlete may understand why a coach prioritizes specific values and principles, but their own values will still inform their principles and resulting behaviors.

Consequently, prescribing the team's values may mean team members struggle to establish common expectations for how they will engage with one another. Determining a set of team values in collaboration with team members is a more inclusive approach to establishing shared expectations. However, it is unlikely that every team member will agree to prioritize the same values. A decision based on the majority opinion becomes necessary. Consequently, this collectively developed set of values creates an illusion that all team members are aligned and requires some team members to conform to the majority's priorities.

You may be thinking, "Hold on, they chose to join the team, so they should buy into the team's values!" As coaches, if we are invested in equitable practices and creating a team in which members view diversity as an asset, a shared set of team values stands in the way of putting this investment into practice. Our values inform our priorities. What matters most to us informs our everyday behaviors. Principles could also be described as personal or professional "guidelines" (Vealey & Chase, 2016).

For example, trust may be one team member's value. So, one of their principles may be that they will follow through on their promises so others know they can trust their word. According to the Golden Rule, which is taught in many American primary schools and through several religious teachings (articulated in different but similar ways), we should treat others as we want to be treated. So, because trust is important to them, they have developed a personal principle that they hope will enable others to trust them.

Here's the thing. Trust contributes to collaboration among team members (Barczak et al., 2010). However, one teammate's approach to demonstrating trustworthiness may or may not be consistent with what another teammate needs to trust them. Additionally, although trust may matter to them, it may not be one of their top values. Accountability could be higher on the list. It may be less important that a teammate follows through with every promise and more important that their friend takes responsibility when they can't follow through with a promise. Building a relationship in which both teammates feel seen and supported means they must discuss their principles and values and what they mean to them. They shift from trying to treat others as we want to be treated and instead adopt an alternative rule, the Platinum Rule. The Platinum Rule invites us to treat others how *they* want to be treated (Bennett, 1979; Rhymes, n.d.).

Our personal experiences, such as what we have been taught is right or wrong, our observations of social interactions, and the impact of social interactions contribute to determining our principles and values. So, our principles and values may indicate how we want to feel and how we want others to feel. Say a person values respect. Respect for others may have become a central value because their teachers told them they should treat others respectfully. Perhaps they were harmed by a person who made a discriminatory comment about their racial identity and do not wish for themselves or others to experience that harm. Maybe they observed a teammate physically bullying a smaller teammate and were upset by seeing someone else experience harm. They may not want anyone to endure a similar experience. They may have experienced feeling respected, as well. For example, their team member asked them about the family they grew up with, not assuming they grew up in a two-parent household, and listened with openness and curiosity as they shared about being raised by their grandmother. As a result of all these interactions, the athlete may prioritize demonstrating respect toward others.

Acting intentionally is essential for coaction; it is important to consider if the actions we choose to engage in enable us to have the impact we want. However, intent does not ensure impact. We can intend to be supportive and not be perceived that way if the "support" does not match what the receiver needs (Haber et al., 2007).

So, what happens when we join a team? Every person is unique, and not all members will have the same values and principles. As a coach, you have a choice. You may express power over team members by determining the principles and values you want to guide your team. This sends a message to the team about what they need to do to comply with your expectations. Relationship-focused values such as trust and respect can encourage team members to work together. However, stating values does not translate to action. Athletes may have different values that can also inform and add complexity to guidelines for how to interact respectfully with others.

Alternatively, you may express power with team members by inviting everyone to share their principles and values. You can wind up with a long, varied list. This is an opportunity for your team to discuss how you will work together in a way that values differences. Team members must learn about and from others with different perspectives and needs and develop strategies to effectively collaborate to make the most of differences as they support one another and work toward shared goals. Do not mistake conformity or homogeneity for connection; connection should not require sameness. Unity can be found in shared purpose and goals, further discussed in the next section.

Further, values are not static—they are learned and shift over time. For this reason, principles and values are interwoven with the other components of the coactive process. For example, uniqueness may not be a value that comes to mind for a team member when they join the team. They may believe this conflicts with the common adage in American sport discussed previously, "there is no 'I' in team." However, through their interactions with team members, they may appreciate what they learn from the unique perspectives others bring to discussions about team dynamics or new plays.

One effective team activity invites everyone to share one thing they appreciate about a team member apart from their athletic performance.[5] After this activity, a team member might reflect on feeling supported by their teammates, such as how Anastasia puts notes with personalized inspiring quotes in each team members' locker and how Raiya always has an energizing playlist prepared in the locker room on game day. Over time, this team member might come to believe the team should celebrate uniqueness.

Revisit principles and values at the start of the season so new and returning team members can share what is necessary to feel supported. Revisiting principles and values throughout the season can also be valuable, as people's priorities and needs may shift on a different timeline than the team's season. Chapter 5, "Co-Creating Purpose," provides practical recommendations for discussing team members' principles and values and how to account for individual differences and commonalities as everyone works collaboratively.

Politics and Purpose

Sport teams exist within various contexts; the team may be part of a larger organization like a university. In the United States, a team is also situated within a city, county, state, and country. These spheres have policies guiding what is expected and permissible for community members. For example, within the National Collegiate Athletic Association (NCAA), a coach can have a team handbook outlining rules for the athletes on their team, the athletic department has policies for all athletes and coaches in the department, and the NCAA has policies for all college athletic departments within each division. Additionally, national policies, such as Title IX, apply to college athletic departments. State policies may also influence college athletic department policies, such as recent bans on transgender athletes competing on teams consistent with their gender identity in collegiate athletics,[6] which may conflict or align with the national sport governing body for specific sports. Coaches' and athletes' experiences are influenced by a complex set of policies.

Policies are explicitly stated rules that outline what is or is not allowable; ideology also guides conduct. Ideology is learned in part through everyday behaviors. For example, it may be common practice for members of a women's team to use the term "ladies" to refer to the team: "Let's go, ladies!" is a common cheer. However, some team members may identify as nonbinary, and the term "ladies" becomes exclusionary. Instead, the team members could agree to use more gender-inclusive language, referring to everyone as "team" or by their mascot: "Let's go, team!" or "Let's go, Wildcats!"

Similarly, team members will have diverse sexualities. When invited to a team event, asking members of a men's team to bring their girlfriends or asking members of a women's team to bring their boyfriends only acknowledges heterosexual team members, in addition to assuming that all athletes on the team identify as men or women. Asking team members to bring their partner or significant other includes LGBTQIA+ team members along with heterosexual team members.

In both cases, the exclusive language suggests that LGBTQIA+ people are not on the team. It erases their membership and signals disinterest in recognizing them as their full selves. Exclusive language signals to LGBTQIA+ people that they are unwelcome, while inclusive language acknowledges all team members' diverse gender and sexual identities and indicates they are welcome and supported.

Team members must have a clear, shared understanding of why they are working together to collaborate effectively. They may have shared goals (e.g., winning competitions), but a team's purpose differs from competitive achievement. Consider the following questions:

- What experience would you like to have when you are with team members?
- What experience do you hope other team members will have when they are with you?
- What long-term impact would you like to have on the team and other communities?

Discussing these questions with team members will guide you in identifying your team's purpose. Identifying a purpose can involve discussing why team members joined this team rather than another. Members invest time in their shared work and show up for one another every day. Consequently, if team members strive to express power with one another, a coach or team captain cannot impose their purpose on all team members. Although all teams are impacted by their political context, some may choose to explicitly discuss their political context and identify a purpose that disrupts policies or ideology that they view as limiting or harmful. For example, in 2025, the NCAA banned transgender women from competing in the women's category.[7] A team may take a clear stance in support of transgender athletes by deciding that one of their purposes is creating and modeling an inclusive environment in their team spaces in which all people can play the sport they love on a team that aligns with their gender identity.

Although winning is not the same as purpose, no discussion of purpose can neglect competition. Competitive sport is, well, competitive. When an athlete joins a team, they expect to compete. In collegiate sports, winning competitions is necessary to qualify for conference, regional, and national championships. So, of course, winning is important to team members. However, winning is an outcome of effectively performing athletic skills, not the purpose of being on a team. If the team never won, would joining the team be pointless? What do you, and the rest of the team members, hope everyone will gain regardless of the team's win-loss record?

A clear purpose is necessary for team members to decide how to contribute to the team's work. Without a purpose, a team lacks direction. Team members must co-determine their purpose to accurately account for what team members need to feel valued and supported. Practical recommendations for collaboratively determining your team's purpose are provided in Chapter 5, "Co-Creating Purpose."

Practices

Once team members discuss the relationships among their values and principles and determine their purpose, they can identify the practices that will help them achieve their purpose while acting in alignment with various members' values and principles. This is a critical step. As noted above, team members may have different ideas about how each member can or should contribute to helping the team achieve their purpose. This is an opportunity to discuss how team members contribute to their work together based on their strengths and who they are. Just as athletes who play different positions on the field do not contribute to gameplay in the same way, team members do not have to engage in the same actions to contribute to the shared experience team members want to have.

Discussing examples of specific actions team members can take to demonstrate their principles and values and contribute to the team's purpose enables them to develop shared expectations for working together. As mentioned in the explanation of values, allocating time to revisit practices throughout the season is valuable. When the team meets to do this, encourage identifying when practices were used and re-evaluating their effectiveness. As team members learn from their experience, they may discover new beneficial practices and add them to the team's expectations.

For example, at the beginning of the season, some athletes may prioritize "catching teammates doing good" to ensure they consistently affirm team members' contributions. One way might be to designate time to post affirmations on lockers at the end of each practice. However, by mid-season, the athletes could become habituated to paying more attention to teammates' contributions and celebrating them. They may readily share these affirmations verbally throughout practice. Team members may also share that they appreciate the real-time feedback. So, athletes may prioritize real-time verbal affirmations rather than posting affirmations on lockers. You'll find practical recommendations for collaboratively identifying team practices in Chapter 6, "Building a Foundation through Alignment, Not Sameness."

Social Identities and Intersectionality

As discussed in the section about the self, all your team members are multifaceted. A person's social identities are part of their self. These identities include but are not limited to sex, gender, race, ethnicity, sexuality, nationality, ability, and religion. Your team members will have different social identities. Additionally, some may share the same social identities, but the salience of the identities may vary, or they might attach different meanings to them. As a coach, you can learn about athletes' self-ascribed identities and how they shape their sense of self. Understanding this can enable you to engage in person-centered coaching. I elaborate on these ideas in Chapter 3, "Cultivating Coaction through Valuing Team Members as Their Full Selves."

The meaning of social identities will vary among team members, while ideology, policies, and everyday practices create and perpetuate inequitable opportunities for members of specific social identity groups to express their power. Some groups are afforded privilege (e.g., people identifying as men, white, heterosexual) and can exercise power without, or with minimal, criticism or consequences. In contrast, others are minoritized and marginalized (e.g., women, BIPOC, LGBTQIA+ people).[8]

Kimberlé Crenshaw's concept of intersectionality provides a tool to examine how inequitable distribution of power functions along intersecting axes of oppression (Bowleg; 2008; Crenshaw, 1989; Collins & Bilge, 2016). For example, a Black lesbian woman does not experience racism, homonegativity, or sexism separately. Instead, all her social identities simultaneously shape her everyday experiences, so they are all implicated in the harm she may experience. Considering a person's experience of one of their social identities without accounting for their other identities does not provide an accurate picture. Instead, it diminishes the complexity of their lived experiences and the social systems they navigate (Bowleg, 2013). Analyzing a single social identity category also reinforces categories because it narrows the scope of examination to a narrow aspect of identity. This approach may also lead to the assumption that everyone with a specific social identity has the same experiences.

As coaches, we can use intersectionality to consider how power affects athletes' experiences. Throughout their lives, athletes have had varied opportunities to express their power within as power to. Those who have had ample opportunities to express their power to are likely to be confident contributors to team efforts. Those who have not had such opportunities or who have experienced negative consequences when attempting to exercise power may be hesitant to assert themselves. As we consider athletes' inclinations, enthusiasm, hesitance, or resistance to actively engaging actions associated with leadership on our teams, we must consider how lived experiences, shaped by social identities, impact their behavior.

Which athletes on your team are most comfortable engaging in traditional, hierarchical leadership behaviors, such as directing teammates or making a decision on behalf of the team? Which athletes are least comfortable? How might engaging athletes in the co-construction of team expectations enable more team members to express their power within as power with team members? We explore these questions throughout this book.

Coaction

Together, the interwoven threads that represent the self and ropes that represent power, values and principles, politics and purpose, and practices comprise the coactive process. Psychologists Dr. Karen L. Suyemoto and Dr. Mary Ballou (2007) describe coaction as:

> a feminist understanding of "leadership" that aims to integrate intersections of multiple oppressions and resist the effects and enactments of these oppressions. Therefore, coaction must value the experience of relational mutuality and prioritize commitment to creating social change for liberation.
>
> (p. 48)

This explanation presents coaction as a form of leadership. However, if a team fully engages in coaction, the leader-follower distinction no longer exists. A core tenet of coaction is that everyone participates equitably. Every person who collaboratively engages in action alongside their teammates is a coactor. I invite you to consider the following questions as you read this book: If I am invested in engaging all team members in effective collaboration, how might focusing on developing *leaders* limit my ability to do so? How might shifting from *developing leaders* to *developing a coactive team* lead to equitable engagement of all team members in our work?

Coaction involves working toward liberation, or "the act or process of freeing someone or something from another's control: the act of liberating someone or something" (Encyclopædia Britannica, n.d.). In traditional leadership, the hierarchical structure encourages leaders to express power over others rather than working toward liberation. Keep in mind that exerting power does not mean a person intends to control others or inflict harm (although sometimes this is the case). Power over can look like prioritizing one's ideas, needs, or goals over another's. In contrast, on a team that engages in coaction, coactors express power with one another.

The coaction model is rooted in recognizing individuality, valuing differences, and investing in working in solidarity with others to achieve mutually beneficial goals, particularly equity and justice. Consequently, coaction is not merely a more inclusive form of leadership. Instead, it offers a more inclusive alternative to leadership, enabling us to imagine a more equitable way of working together.

Rather than expecting team members to conform to imposed expectations of what leadership requires, coactors want them to express their whole, unique selves. Every team member has different perspectives and strengths. Diverse perspectives and strengths enable team members to stretch their perspectives and develop creative, well-thought-out methods for working together. Each individual can contribute their strengths toward the team's shared goals.

Coaction also enables team members to adapt to the current circumstances since they do not possess the singular role of "leader" or "follower." Coactors engage in coordinated actions at specific moments. At times, one team member may provide direction. However, they do not hold a superior status; this directing position is not permanent. At another point, the same team member may step back so another team member can take on a directing role. Team members' actions and roles are responsive to teammates' needs and what will best support the team's shared work.

Throughout this book, I guide you through methods of teaching athletes to engage in coaction and engaging in coaction with them. Coaction is an equity-centered, person-first, and trauma-informed approach to interacting with others. It requires learning from each person about who they are rather than trying to determine whether they fit into expected roles. Engaging in coaction lets you and your team members co-determine how to support one another best. Coaction means all athletes can recognize their capacity, contribute their strengths to team efforts, and develop their skills as inclusive collaborators.

Self-Determination Theory

Understanding factors affecting athletes' motivation to actively engage in coaction is essential for supporting their development. In discussing intersectionality, I considered how social structures impact athletes' opportunities to express power. Now, we turn to everyday interactions between coaches and athletes and among athletes.

Coaches often expect athletes to be self-motivated to develop as leaders because leadership is valued within sport culture and, more broadly, in American society. However, Self-Determination Theory indicates that intrinsic motivation, or motivation from within oneself, does not happen on its own (Deci & Ryan, 1985). Instead, every person has three psychological needs:

- A sense of competence—the belief that they have skills and the ability to develop those skills further,
- A sense of autonomy—the belief that they have control in their lives, the ability to make decisions, and the ability to contribute to collaborative decisions, and
- A sense of relatedness—a feeling of connectedness with others, feeling valued by community members.

The fulfillment of each of these needs contributes to intrinsic motivation.

If an athlete's psychological needs are not met, why would they be interested in engaging in coaction? Furthermore, if they have learned that leadership consists of a specific skill set, don't believe they have the skills to be a leader, or lack opportunities to develop leadership skills, they will have difficulty imagining themselves as competent leaders. If an athlete cannot make decisions for themselves or contribute to team decisions, they will struggle to believe they are a capable decision-maker. Someone habituated to following directions may not even believe they know what is best for themselves. If an athlete doesn't feel like a valued team member or see people that they relate to receive recognition as leaders, they may not believe other people would perceive them as a leader.

Coaction relies on team members' unique strengths; coaction cannot exist if everyone is the same. Prioritizing coaction frees athletes from the pressure to prove themselves as leaders. Instead, the question becomes, "What unique perspective and skills do you bring, and how can we create opportunities for you to apply them to support the team?" Rather than emulating model leaders, coactors collaborate and expand their skill sets as they learn from one another.

As a coach, your interactions can support or thwart the fulfillment of athletes' three psychological needs. If you intentionally meet athletes' psychological needs, you contribute to their intrinsic motivation to engage in coaction. Throughout this book, I provide practical recommendations that enable you to help fulfill these needs. Additionally, your actions show athletes how they can support one another. As a result, all team members can experience intrinsic motivation to engage in coaction.

Polyvagal Theory

Polyvagal Theory offers a way of understanding the importance of a person's sense of safety. Athletes' sense of safety, or lack thereof, impacts if and how they engage with their team members. According to Porges and Porges (2023),

> When we feel safe, we are capable of generosity, empathy, altruism, growth, and compassion.

When we don't (or perhaps never) feel safe, our sense of self-preservation trumps all else, and selfish, desperate, and aggressive behaviors are all but inevitable for most people.

(pp. xix–xx)

When we feel unsafe, our nervous system goes into what is known as "fight or flight" (including the less frequently mentioned "freeze" and "fawn" responses) or, in extreme circumstances, engages the dorsal vagal complex. When that happens, we are more likely to engage in behaviors that can include anti-social tendencies and experiences such as dissociation, depression, "feeling stuck" or disconnected from self, or destructive behaviors that can be a result of the attempt to re-regulate our nervous system, cope, or feel.

On the other hand, a sense of safety facilitates pro-social behaviors because feeling safe prompts a physical and psychological response. Our nervous system engages the ventral vagal complex, which creates feelings of relaxation, engagement, curiosity, creativity, and hopefulness (Polyvagal Institute, 2023). With this in mind, developing a coactive team depends on cultivating an environment where team members feel safe. Prioritizing coaction facilitates an essential sense of safety.

You may remember that Batliwala pointed out that leadership encourages competition; to obtain a superior position over others, you must prove that you are superior to them. Competition can thus create a sense of threat. What happens if I am not good enough to be a leader? What happens if I don't become a leader? I have two options: continuously try to prove myself or accept my role as a follower.

As a coactor, each team member is viewed as inherently valuable. The onus is not on them to prove themselves worthy of a particular social status. Instead, team members meet them with curiosity about what they would like to share. Together, coacting team members can explore and identify how their strengths and areas for growth fit together like puzzle pieces. Coaction is a creative process.

Sometimes, pieces might not quite fit together or a piece may be missing. Rather than depending on a leader to determine how to address these challenges, team members can explore possibilities and experiment with solutions to discover the most effective response. This strengths-focused, creative approach contributes to athletes' sense of safety, feeding back into cultivating a coactive team.

This is not to say that team members will never engage in disruptive behaviors or have conflicts with one another. Instead, when such behaviors or conflicts arise, coactors have the skills to approach the challenge with curiosity and a problem-solving mentality rather than blame and shame.[9]

Tying It All Together

Every sport team can determine how they want to work together. Some team members may be inclined to engage in traditional leadership practices because that is what they are most familiar with. However, through intentional, proactive dialogue, team members can reflect on and share their experiences, values, and personal needs. In doing so, team members can develop a more inclusive way of working together that accounts for their diverse needs and strengths. Engaging in this process shifts the team structure from hierarchical leadership, in which only a few team members are privileged as leaders, to a network-like structure that enables all team members to be coactors.

Engaging in coaction requires consistently paying attention to power dynamics among team members. In particular, coaction highlights that everyone has power. As coaches, taking this into account helps us see ourselves not as the givers of power but rather as coactors who can encourage and enable athletes to use their power. We can intentionally express power with athletes to allow them to express their power and encourage athletes to do the same with one another. Additionally, while we may need to assign specific roles, these should be purposeful and rotated among team members. Giving specific athletes long-term roles encourages other team members to comply. Rotating responsibility creates more possibility for development and coaction.

Further, as we've discussed, traditional hierarchical leadership models only affirm the leadership abilities of a few team members. Engaging in coaction provides ongoing opportunities for all team members to celebrate one another's competence by expressing appreciation for their contributions and providing opportunities for development.

Polyvagal Theory helps us understand the conditions required for a person to connect with others, while Self-Determination Theory helps us understand how team members can facilitate or thwart a person's motivation to engage in coaction. Coacting enables autonomy by involving team members in decision-making about their needs and how they will work toward the team's purpose.

Through experiences of affirmation and opportunities for involvement, coacting team members' sense of competence and relatedness can be fulfilled. When team members' psychological needs are fulfilled, they are more likely to be self-motivated to engage in coaction. Once coaction becomes the expected way of working together on your team, it becomes a continuous feedback loop. Team members contribute to one another's sense of safety, become more inclined to engage with others, and are motivated to explore how they can effectively apply their strengths and adapt as they work toward achieving the team's purpose and goals.

Notes

1 Pseudonym.

2 For some examples, see Transformational Leadership and Servant Leadership.

3 I use the terms "group" and "team" intentionally throughout this book. As John Amaechi (2021) explains, people who are part of a group or a team may be working toward a shared goal with other members of the group or team. However, in a group, members work individually, focused on completing their own tasks. They interact with one another when necessary. On a team, members are invested in working collaboratively and supporting one another's efforts.

4 For an example of this, see ESPN (2013).

5 See *Finished It: A Team's Journey to Winning it All* for further explanation of the compliment bag activity.

6 For more information, visit Transathlete.com: www.transathlete.com/take-action

7 For more information about the current policy, see www.ncaa.org/sports/2022/1/27/transgender-participation-policy.aspx

8 The Power Wheel created by the Canadian Council for Refugees provides a visual explanation of different social groups' ability to express their *power to*, afforded by privilege: https://ccrweb.ca/en/anti-oppression

9 As a coach, you have the responsibility to draw the line and name that the support an athlete needs extends beyond your professional role and training, and then refer the athlete to a mental health professional. A professional athletic counselor can be a helpful resource for helping you determine the scope of your role as a coach who supports athletes as their whole selves and when you should refer athletes to an athletic counselor.

References

Barczak, G., Lassk, F., & Mulki, J. (2010). Antecedents of team creativity: An examination of team emotional intelligence, team trust and collaborative culture. *Creativity & Innovation Management, 19*, 332–345. https://doi.org/10.1111/j.1467-8691.2010.00574.x

Bass, B. M. (1985). *Leadership and performance beyond expectations*. Free Press.

Batliwala, S. (2011). *Feminist leadership for social transformation: Clearing the conceptual cloud*. Crea.

Batliwala, S. (2019). *All about Power: Understanding social power & power structures*. Crea.

Bennett, M.J. (1979) Overcoming the Golden Rule: Sympathy and empathy. In D. Nimmo, D. (Ed.), *Communication Yearbook 3* (pp. 406–422), International Communication Association, Transaction Publishers. https://doi.org/10.1080/23808985.1979.11923774

Bowleg, L. (2008). When Black + lesbian + woman ≠ Black lesbian woman: The methodological challenges of qualitative and quantitative intersectionality research. *Sex Roles*, *59*(5-6), 312–325.

Bowleg, L. (2013). "Once you've blended the cake, you can't take the parts back to the main ingredients": Black gay and bisexual men's descriptions and experiences of intersectionality. *Sex Roles: A Journal of Research, 68*(11-12), 754–767. https://doi.org/10.1007/s11199-012-0152-4

Burns, J. M. (1978). *Leadership*. Harper & Row.

Cain, S. (2013). *Quiet: The power of introverts in a world that can't stop talking*. Crown Publishing Group/Random House.

Collins, P. H. & Bilge, S. (2016). *Intersectionality*. Polity Press.

Crenshaw, K. (1989). Demarginalizing the intersection of race and sex: A black feminist critique of antidiscrimination doctrine, feminist theory and antiracist politics. *University of Chicago Legal Forum, 1989*(1), 139–167. https://chicagounbound.uchicago.edu/uclf/vol1989/iss1/8

Deci, E. L., & Ryan, R. M. (1985). *Intrinsic motivation and self-determination in human behavior*. Plenum Press.

Diamond, L. M., & Alley, J. (2022). Rethinking minority stress: A social safety perspective on the health effects of stigma in sexually-diverse and gender-diverse populations. *Neuroscience & Biobehavioral Reviews, 138*, 1–36. https://doi.org/10.1016/j.neubiorev.2022.104720.

Downton, J. V. (1973). *Rebel leadership: Commitment and charisma in the revolutionary process*. Free Press.

Doyle, G. (Host). (2023, July 13). Megan Rapinoe: A legend says goodbye to the game (No. 227). [audio podcast episode]. In *We Can Do Hard Things*.

Encyclopædia Britannica. (n.d.) liberation. www.britannica.com/dictionary/liberation

ESPN. (2013, May 18). Griner: No talking sexuality at Baylor. ESPN. www.espn.com/wnba/story/_/id/9289080/brittney-griner-says-baylor-coach-kim-mulkey-told-players-keep-quiet-sexuality

Evans, A. B., & Pfister, G. U. (2021). Women in sports leadership: A systematic narrative review. *International Review for the Sociology of Sport, 56*(3), 317–342. https://doi.org/10.1177/1012690220911842

Fletcher, L. & Marvell, R. (2023) Furthering transgender inclusion in the workplace: Advancing a new model of allyship intentions and perceptions. *International Journal of Human Resource Management, 34*(9), 1726–1756. https://doi.org/10.1080/09585192.2021.2023895

Gino, F., Sezer, O., Huang, L. (2020). To be or not to be your authentic self? Catering to others' preferences hinders performance. *Organizational Behavior and Human Decision Processes, 158*, 83–100. https://doi.org/10.1016/j.obhdp.2020.01.003

Greenleaf, R. K. (1970). *The servant as leader.* Robert K. Greenleaf Publishing Center.

Haber, M. G., Cohen, J. L., Lucas, T., Baltes, B. B. (2007). The relationship between self-reported received and perceived social support: A meta-analytic review. *American Journal of Community Psychology, 39*(1-2), 133–44. https://doi.org/10.1007/s10464-007-9100-9

Heywood L. L. (2011). Affective infrastructures: Toward a cultural neuropsychology of sport. *Frontiers in Evolutionary Neuroscience, 3*(4), 1–5. https://doi.org/10.3389%2Ffnevo.2011.00004

Line, Jo. (2021). Using a feminist approach to leadership education to promote coaction among women collegiate student-athletes. In K. N. LaVenia & J. Jackson May (Eds.) *Case studies in leadership and adult development: Applying theoretical perspectives to real world challenges* (pp. 131–139). Taylor & Francis.

Polyvagal Institute. (2023). *Polyvagal Institute autonomic nervous system Polyvagal Theory diagram graphic.* www.polyvagalinstitute.org/whatispolyvagaltheory?lightbox=dataItem-lhanzl12

Porges, S. W. (1995). Orienting in a defensive world: Mammalian modifications of our evolutionary heritage. A Polyvagal Theory. *Psychophysiology, 32*(4), 301–18. https://doi.org/10.1111/j.1469-8986.1995.tb01213.x

Porges, S. W. & Porges, S. (2023). *Our polyvagal world: How safety and trauma change us.* W. W. Norton.

Rhymes, S. (n.d.). *5 ways to use the Platinum Rule at work: Do unto others...* InHerSight. www.inhersight.com/blog/culture-and-professionalism/platinum-rule

Suyemoto, K. L., & Ballou, M. B. (2007). Conducted monotones to coacted harmonies: A feminist (re)conceptualization of leadership addressing race, class, and gender. In J. L. Chin, B. Lott, J. K. Rice, & J. Sanchez-Hucles (Eds.), *Women and leadership: Transforming visions and diverse voices* (pp. 35–54). Blackwell Publishing.

Taylor, J. (2016, September 7). *Build a team culture of athletic success.* Psychology Today. www.psychologytoday.com/us/blog/the-power-prime/201609/build-team-culture-athletic-success

Vealey, R. S., & Chase, M. A. (2016). *Best practice for youth sport.* Human Kinetics.

VeneKlasen, L., & Miller, V. (2002). *Power and empowerment.* PLA Notes, *43*, 39–41.

3 Cultivating Coaction through Valuing Team Members as Their Full Selves

The Self is represented by the threads that construct each rope in the braid of the coactive process. A team begins to form when individuals decide to come together to achieve something they cannot do alone, but what makes a team coactive is team members accounting for how every aspect of the coactive process is impacted by and impacts every individual. The Self includes:

- personality
- self-esteem
- history, experience
- talents
- abilities
- inclinations
- identities (Batliwala, 2011).

A person cannot pick and choose what parts of themselves they bring to practice or competitions. They are a whole, complex person all the time. However, the question is: does each member feel safe enough to share their whole self with the team, or do they feel like they must manage what they communicate to fit what the team deems "normal" or "ideal"? The standards for how a team member should present themselves, express their identities, and behave can discourage or encourage self-expression.

For example, let's return to the adage "there is no 'I' in team." The intent behind the adage may be to discourage selfishness rather than suppress individual expression. However, let's take a critical look at this idea:

DOI: 10.4324/9781003605485-3

- Have you asked individual members to take on responsibilities to support the team?
- Have individual members been assigned specific responsibilities due to their unique assets?
- Do you aim to support each athlete's learning by adjusting how you teach specific skills?
- Do you ask team members to share questions or concerns, even if they require individual discussions?

If you answered yes to any of these questions, you recognize the individuality of every team member. If athletes believe they are expected to put the team before themselves, though, what might they not share about who they are or what they need? Might they fear being perceived as selfish?

As we saw in Chapter 2, "The New Framework: The Coactive Process," every individual has psychological needs that require support from others. What might our team dynamic feel and look like if, at the beginning of the season, we said:

> Actually, there is an 'I' in team. Each one of you is a valuable member as you are. Our differences strengthen our team, so we will recognize and celebrate them. Together, we can strategize how to make the most of the diverse assets you each have to contribute. We will also expand our skills by learning from one another?

Several athletes in my study stated that anyone can be a leader and that there are many ways a person can lead. I did not ask these athletes about coaction, but their description of leadership suggested that many team members can be involved in it, which closely aligns with coaction. For example, Mina stated,

> I think every leader has a leader, so everyone's a leader and everyone's a follower. You always look up to someone, which makes you a follower of that person. So, it depends on the situation. I'm probably a leader to someone, but I have six or seven leaders that I look up to. I bet they also have leaders that they look up to.

Mina highlights that different team members will view different people as role models. When team members feel safe and encouraged to show up as their full selves, they have many unique role models they can relate to or be inspired by. Visibility creates possibilities. If a select few team members are celebrated as leaders, who may be overlooked or undercelebrated?

Although athletes indicated that there are many ways a person could lead, several described leaders as providing support and guidance. They discussed role models who inspire them due to the care they demonstrate or the encouragement the athletes observed them offering others. This care requires recognizing individuals as their unique and complex selves and supporting them in the way they need. For example, Jackie explained that she views her mom as a leader.

> She'll always say, "In the military, I taught class, and if anyone ever didn't understand something, I would show them. Sometimes, you have to remember that even though other people don't get it, you can't get frustrated with them because that just makes them even more frustrated, and then nothing gets accomplished." So, she's a really good people person, she's a really good leader.

Providing support and guidance, when done with attention to what the recipient needs, is a way of expressing power with someone. The person providing support and guidance is also being guided by the recipient, so they take the most helpful approach. This shifts the relationship dynamic from that of leader-follower to that of coactors. Coactors demonstrate care through actions.

Every person on your team has assets they can contribute now. Whether or not a team member is an active contributor is not simply a matter of choice; a person's engagement depends on recognition of their abilities and opportunities given (or denied) to be a valued contributor. Consequently, everyday interactions among team members and the team culture support or stifle athletes' growth as coactors.

In this chapter, we focus on cultivating athletes' sense of safety and support so they can explore, share, and experience validation of who they are. Creating an environment where athletes feel safe to be their whole selves is foundational for creating a coactive team. For guidance, we hear from coaches and athletes about how team members' visibility has impacted others. Stories from coaches and athletes offer examples of how they demonstrate care through their actions and the ways these actions have impacted team members. Research from psychology, sociology, Asian American studies, and disability studies explains why visibility creates possibilities and the outcomes that demonstrating care through actions makes possible.

Visibility Creates Possibilities (or Risks)

Lived experiences, particularly how we feel in response to how others treat us, can inform how we aim to impact others. For example, Coach Kadine Johnson-Crowder discussed coaches who inspired her and harmful experiences that inform why and how she coaches. Coach Johnson-Crowder explained:

> What inspired me was the treatment that I experienced. [In] high school, … I had two amazing coaches: my head coach, Andy Capellan from New Rochelle High School. That man is a blessing to every athlete that has ever crossed his path. And my throws coach, Natalia Brown. She threw discus for Jamaica. She was a very hardworking, determined, just amazing individual, and she poured into people. So, coming out of high school, experiencing that the journey itself wasn't easy, but the way that they supported and showed love, it was new to me.

This experience did not continue throughout Coach Johnson-Crowder's athletic or coaching career. She explained that when she began coaching, it became clear that she was not supported as her full self:

> So, I get into that space [as a coach], and I realize, "Oh, the toxicities!" This is real, I'm navigating, I'm fighting, I'm doing everything that I possibly can. I end up bouncing around literally the country for probably the next 10 years. Roughly, a little bit more. And it didn't click that a part of what I was fighting was the fact that I am a Black woman in a space where it's very male dominant, and it doesn't really help that I am, how they say "melanatedly advanced," or I have a deeper set of melanin. They didn't really like that. It became very clear very quickly that if I was to be in those spaces, I had to make sure that, optically, I was number two. I didn't get it because I thought the concept as an assistant coach is okay, you have a coach for throws, you have a coach for jumps, you have a coach for sprints. We're all trying to get our athletes to be the best that they possibly can.

You may recall from the introduction to this book that 5% of head coaches of NCAA teams are women of color. This low percentage is not due to a lack of interest or qualifications but rather systemic barriers and a lack of support limiting their opportunities and the sustainability of their coaching careers (LaVoi & Dutove, 2012). If athletes are told they should be leaders, but few people in leadership roles share their identities, why would they envision themselves as leaders? If they see people they relate to in leadership roles facing ongoing harm, why would they believe they can hold these positions and thrive?

Cultivating a culture of mutual support on a team where all members believe they can be fully visible as themselves requires everyone, not just those in formal leadership roles. As an athlete, yoga instructor, and personal trainer, KC observed teammates engaging in homophobic behaviors, which discouraged them from expressing their full self.

> I had already come to the conclusion that I was queer in high school, but I wasn't out yet, and there was one girl on the team that was out, and it was just like once she came out, the whole team was very worried about her being in the locker room. I remember that, for a long time, I was like, "Well, I can never come out because I could never go through [that]. I don't want people talking about me like that. I don't want them to be threatened by me like that." I think that definitely held the team back in general because then I'm not showing up fully, and that isn't great for them. It's not great for anybody, so that was definitely a barrier to inclusivity at the time, ...the late 2000s, early 2010s. I graduated high school in 2011. Those years were just tough, more tough on .... queer people in general... You just didn't have people showing up as their authentic selves. And that just halts people's life force energy, which is so, so important when it comes to movement.

Harm occurs directly, and it shows up in subtler ways, as KC describes. As discussed in Chapter 2, the social environment affects a person's sense of safety. If a team member feels that they must conceal an aspect of who they are, this will hinder their sense of safety. KC's experience also highlights that visibility comes with risk; not only did KC's teammate directly experience harm, but the discrimination she faced from teammates discouraged KC from being fully visible. Team members must intentionally demonstrate support and disrupt and prevent harm to enable everyone to be visible safely.

Even when the team is invested in creating a safe environment, it is possible that athletes may not disclose everything about themselves, and they should not be required to do so. Sharing your whole self can be difficult and exhausting if you are the only person, or one of a few, within a community with your identities, experiences, or perspectives. Sharing may involve risk for staff members and athletes with minoritized identities. As Dr. Carey Yazeed (2021) explained, not all members within a group are equally safe disclosing aspects of their identities, sharing their experiences, or stating their perspectives. For example, some people may treat a Black woman as disruptive for calling out racism or sexism on her team, and she might face disciplinary action for naming discriminatory behaviors or structures. In this case, she may remain silent to avoid further harm.

Coach Johnson-Crowder offered an example of how team members can be encouraged to fully express who they are and how this supports their well-being, as KC suggested it would.

> Athletics allows people to navigate certain neurodivergence simply because of how it presents itself to the world. So, if you are constantly moving and fidgeting, and the first thing somebody says to you [is], "Oh, my gosh! You need to sit still"... But that movement and fidgeting and all the energy is praised on the court, is praised on the field, is praised on the track, you're going to feel drawn to an area that praises you for who you are, whether you recognize that that's what's happening or not. I can tell you... at least ... 90% of my team are neurodivergent. All walks. And with that, they have come to terms with who they are because they see me saying, "Yeah!"
>
> They're like, "You have autism?"
>
> "Mmhm."
>
> They're like, "For real?"
>
> "Yeah, autism, ADHD, constantly duking it out up here. Have no clue what's going to happen next, but here we are."
>
> "Then how'd you graduate?"
>
> "I fought for it."
>
> ...They'll talk about my Master's [degree]. "But you went back to school."
>
> ..."Yeah, under my own terms. I went back to school knowing that me typing up essays traditionally wasn't gonna happen. ...

> I had to do audio, so I had to speak every essay and then go through and edit it."
>
> But to sit there and type… I have dyslexia, dysgraphia. So, it was stressful and straining to do that. I was like, "Okay, if we're gonna do this. I have to do this my way."
>
> Still had no clue what was going on. But I was like, "I'm gonna get this degree."
>
> So, to them now, they see some of these pieces. They see me navigating. They see me having stim attacks when I'm super overstimulated, overwhelmed, and I'm like, "I need a second," and I'm in a corner shaking. I have athletes coming over, and they're like rubbing my back. They're like, "You got this coach," because… I'm not gonna hide who I am. Nor am I going to be ashamed. I was born this way. I was made this way. I'm not going to be ashamed of the way I came out the womb, m-m, but a lot of them struggle with it.

Coach Johnson-Crowder is a role model for athletes on her team and for people outside of sport environments. Coach Johnson-Crowder proudly expresses her neurodivergence, and she shares her needs with her team members, showing athletes that even people in leadership roles need support. This need for support includes neurotypical athletes as well. Allowing athletes to support her is a way of expressing power with them. Athletes do not just receive guidance; they contribute to a culture of mutual support. By seeing everyone give and receive support, athletes are encouraged to practice self-acceptance and to express who they are. Coach Johnson-Crowder continued,

> So, I had athletes who are autistic, but saying that they have ADHD is a little bit easier or doesn't feel as judgey. And now you ask them, and they're like, "My bad coach. 'Tism moment. My bad, hold on, I didn't mean it like that." They claim it. They live in it. They know, "Okay, maybe I have to step away 'cause this is overstimulating." Maybe we have to have a quiet practice. Maybe this is gonna be a practice where everything's bouncing off the walls cause we gotta get this energy out. We acclimate, and… I've noticed they're more willing to go to disability services to ask for help. So, now they're like, "I think something's going on. I don't know what, but I've been talking to my coach, and she said the best bet is for me to come in and talk to you guys. So, I think

something's happening." Next thing you know, they have extended time. They have referrals… to get professionally assessed, like a trickle-down effect.

…Even for the individuals who might not be neurodivergent, they now get to see accurate representation of what neurodivergence actually looks like. Because if you let media tell it, people with autism aren't intellectuals, or they physically present restricted from the world, but they're brilliant on the inside. And those… representations of autism and ADHD do exist in the world. But those aren't the only ones. And what oftentimes happens is, you have people who will say, "You're autistic. I would never guess, you're so smart. You're so well-spoken. Oh, my goodness! What? You never! You couldn't be." And it doesn't mean we're not intelligent. We just experience the world differently. So that now for me is huge, because the neurotypical population gets a chance to see us exist in real life, real-time, and get a true understanding of what that looks like, so that they can now move subconsciously or consciously, more aware. So, it's kind of like a win-win.

Coach Johnson-Crowder, expressing her authentic self and needs, supports athletes' sense of safety, showing them that they can also be their full selves and ask for support. Her visibility creates possibilities on their team and in the classroom. Visibility also includes modeling how to support one's own needs and the needs of team members.

Athletes Bailey and Kenza also pointed out the power of visibility within sport, within and beyond one's own team.

Bailey: [My coach] ran in high school. I look up to her style, and she works hard and puts 110% into everything that she does as a coach. Then, she talks about how she did with her sports and academics. She would tell me always to follow my heart, and it influenced the person I am today. I can see it being that she is a woman coach, too. Her being a woman, working towards stuff, it's kind of inspiring. She was the only woman coach I've had. I had two other coaches who were men.

Kenza: I grew up watching Tennessee basketball a lot because of Coach Pat Summit and the athletes on her team, particularly Candace Parker and Isabelle Harrison. Watching those girls and seeing how good they were—they didn't have to be guys; they had just as much talent. They don't have to pack the muscles or do a bunch of slam dunks to be just as good. Watching them, I could see how fundamentally good they were playing basketball. I didn't have to do all the showboating. If I want entertainment, I can go watch the guys catch alley-oops and stuff like that. I watch women's basketball to learn from it. I know I can do it because they're women athletes.

Freshman year of high school, I knew I wanted to play college basketball. Watching Candace Parker, I just wanted to follow in her footsteps. She is a leader on the floor, a great basketball player, and she seemed like a great teammate just from watching. I could tell that's somebody I want to play with. She just impacted my life as a young basketball player. She was and still is my favorite basketball player. I wanted to go to Tennessee; I wanted to play for Pat Summit. I wanted to wear number three. I was kinda heartbroken when we didn't have number three in high school, so I was like, "All right, I'm gonna wear number 23 just like Maya Moore. We're gonna try to stay on track."

I think we kinda gravitate to the LeBrons and look for men athletes, but as a woman, Candace Parker was the first woman athlete that I was like, "I want to be just like her." Then after a while watching her, it became Maya Moore, and then it's like instead of me wanting to be LeBron or James Harden, I can look up to these women and want to be just like them. I will watch a WNBA game over NBA just because those are the people I look up to and want to be like someday and reach their level of success. I don't know them personally, but watching them growing up, I could say they impacted the way I play basketball and watch basketball. I love basketball and want to play post-collegiately because I watched them have fun with the sport. Candace Parker's actions made me want to inspire others the way she's inspired me.

Bailey and Kenza's stories emphasize that visibility creates possibilities. Kenza shared that Candace Parker, Isabelle Harrison, and Maya Moore demonstrated that women of color can lead in sport, and seeing them excel inspired her to pursue playing basketball in college, too. Bailey also had a supportive woman coach, who became a role model. While visibility creates possibilities by indicating that a person can express their full selves, they must also be supported by those around them to do so safely. This requires team members to be intentional about their actions.

Demonstrating Care through Actions

As discussed earlier in this chapter, assuming a leadership role does not ensure that a person has a positive impact on others. Without attention to intentions and actions, which will be discussed further in Chapter 6, "Building a Foundation through Alignment, Not Sameness," coaches may inadvertently constrain the possibilities that athletes envision for themselves. Athlete Nicole shared,

> In high school, the coaches would share responsibilities for the guys' and the girls' teams, so we were always together at practice and meets. I was a captain on the girls' team, and there was a captain on the guys' team. One time one of the guys said it should be easy for the guys to do a workout, but not the girls. I was like, "No, just because you guys are guys doesn't mean the girls can't do it."
>
> The coach was like, "No, you can't do it, you'll get injured, or you'll cry."
>
> I was like, "Fine, the girls are gonna do it with the guys, and we'll see how it works out."
>
> I brought the girls over to the side and said, "All right, this is gonna be a really hard practice, but you need to show the guys that we're not babies."
>
> Everybody had the best workout, and none of the guys were beating the girls. I was up in the top group with all the guys, and my coach was like, "Oh, sorry, I figured you guys couldn't do it."
>
> I was like, "That's so stupid of you to think that. Just because they're guys doesn't mean I can't run with them. That's not very nice, and I don't want to hear you say that again."
>
> My teammates were like, "Yeah!"
>
> It was like a big deal. I remember it because I was like, "I never wanna be put down just because I'm a girl. I'm fast enough to run with guys."

In contrast to Bailey, Nicole had to convince her high school coach that she and her women teammates were as athletically capable as the men. While Nicole had a strong enough sense of her power within to challenge her coach, other women team members may have complied with the coach's assumption that women were not as capable as men due to the coach's position of authority. If Nicole had not intervened, this could have been a discouraging experience for the women athletes and reinforced gender stereotypes for all team members. An athlete should not bear the burden of challenging their coach's discriminatory assumptions. This will likely breed mistrust and hinder a sense of support and safety.

As coaches, we know not all team members will share commonalities in identities or experiences. However, everyone can choose if and how they learn about and respond to these differences. For example, Nicole's coach, described above, chose a limiting and potentially harmful way to respond to perceived differences. He made an assumption about athletic ability based on his perception of binary gender differences. Gender identity does not determine a person's athletic ability; not all people who identify as men run faster than all people who identify as women. Alternatively, he could have considered the individuality of each athlete, focusing on the relevant information for the situation: their current fitness and their sense of preparedness for the workout. To determine paces, he could have looked at athletes' paces from recent competitions. He could have also asked athletes how they were feeling that day, accounting for how rested and fueled they were and their current stress level. Together, he and each athlete could determine their appropriate pace for the day.

A shared love of their sport alone will not facilitate effective coaction. Team members must learn about one another to determine how to best work together. College basketball coach Dawn Staley has discussed the importance of building relationships with the athletes she coaches, and these relationships impact how she coaches. She explained,

> I need to have a personal relationship with each player. I, just like they do, have to be invested. Something other than basketball has to draw me to them. Basketball is the immediate common ground between us, of course, but I'm talking about a personal level. I like to have something more… But after seven years and after building personal relationships with these players—relationships

> that require reciprocal trust and vulnerability—that guard is down. They're seeing more of me—who I really am—than any other place I've been. I'm more myself now. That feeling of letting my guard down allows me to give my all. I credit our players for allowing me to coach the way I do. I don't have to censor anything. I don't have to put on airs. I feel what I feel when I feel it, and then I express it. That's what the people and players of South Carolina have done: help me be myself.
>
> You can't ask a player to let you in if you don't do the same.
>
> (Staley, 2015, para. 15 and 20)

Two years after Coach Staley shared this, the South Carolina Women's Basketball Team won their first national championship, and two additional national championship titles have followed since.

Although this book is not here to give you quick strategies to win games, coaction can contribute to winning. However, we are focused on creating a team culture that enables every member of your team to experience safety, support, and growth throughout their time as an engaged member of your team. Even if your team does not win a national championship (due to the structure of athletic competitions, most teams will not be national champions), your athletes will benefit from being members of your team.

While Coach Staley and Coach Johnson-Crowder discussed modeling the behaviors you expect from athletes, Coach Feldman discussed how consistent alignment between his words and actions contributes to cultivating relationships with the athletes on his team. He shared,

> I think my actions and what gets out dictates how forthcoming anybody on the team is. So, kids will come to me all the time if they're really struggling with something. I think my track record lends to that. I've heard from kids on the team where they really encourage the underclassmen to come to talk to me, because they say that I'm flexible and willing to work with them. And I have a policy that if you come talk to me or send me a text saying, "Hey, I'm really stressed from school or something outside of school. Can I not come to practice?" 99 out of 100 times I'm gonna say, "That's okay. Just get your run in on your own." And I think for a lot of kids, knowing that they have that as an option makes them

feel safe, and if you feel safe, then trust is going to form. And then when trust forms, then there's that communication factor.

Coach Staley and Coach Feldman both note the importance of trust in their relationships with athletes. These coaches explain their intentional actions to demonstrate care, which enables the athletes to feel safe and seen as whole people, not just as athletes. Like Coach Johnson-Crowder, Coach Staley discusses being herself with her athletes so they feel like they can express their whole selves.

Together, Coach Johnson-Crowder, Coach Staley, Coach Feldman, and Bailey's insights emphasize how coaches can build trusting relationships with athletes and the potential impact of these relationships on athletes. Due to their position of authority, how coaches model sharing about themselves will impact athletes' willingness to share their perspectives. As a coach, your behaviors and the information you disclose to athletes signal what is acceptable. As Coach Feldman stated, athletes "know somebody that means what they say, and somebody that might just be all talk." So, if you tell athletes that they can express their whole selves, but you do not share details about your life and experiences, they may hesitate to be open with you. Coach Johnson-Crowder demonstrates that the opposite is also true.

As a coach, you must decide what you are comfortable sharing and what is acceptable. Your professional boundaries matter; your athletes are not your peers. Sometimes, an athlete wants to share something personal with their coach that their coach would not also share. For example, you would not discuss your dating life with an athlete on your team, but an athlete may want to discuss a challenge with someone they are dating. This disclosure is the athlete's choice. However, can you expect an athlete to be comfortable discussing their family with you if you have never talked about your own?

A Team Is More Than a Collection of "I"s

Research on membership within a community involves a combination of individual, interpersonal, and systemic factors. Sociologists Dr. Evelyn Nakano Glenn (2011) and Ali Greey (2022) have shed light on formal and informal aspects of experiencing membership. Within the context of sport, an athlete may become a formal team member by signing up or signing a contract. However, merely joining does not ensure that an athlete will feel like they are a valued team member. This is the informal side of membership within a community.

Greey (2022) applied this understanding of membership to trans peoples' experiences using locker rooms and how these experiences impact their participation in sport and physical activity. In Ontario, Canada, trans people have the right to use a gym locker room aligned with their gender identity. This is a formal, systemic protection. However, the discriminatory behaviors of other gym-goers in the locker room who perceive trans people as a threat create an exclusive environment that discourages them from using this community space, thereby discouraging their participation in physical activity. This is an informal, interpersonal barrier. Locker room mistreatment becomes an individual burden placed on the trans person, who must decide whether they use any public locker room. They may develop strategies as they come and go to the gym to avoid interactions in the locker room. They may even consider whether they continue participating in gym activities. They will not experience what Glenn (2011) and Greey describe as membership unless others demonstrate they are welcome through interpersonal actions, structural and administrative support, and systemic protections.

Applying this understanding of membership more broadly to sport teams, a formal member of a team has the right to access specific resources (e.g., receive coaching, practice, and compete with team-issued equipment, use the team locker room and weight room) and participate in team training and competitions. However, formal membership does not ensure access to those resources and activities, or that the resources provided fully fit their needs. Further, other team members may demonstrate acceptance or deny a person membership and the benefits that come with it through everyday interactions and by providing access to resources they need to fully participate in their sport.

We can apply these ideas to members of other minoritized communities. Coach Johnson-Crowder provides an example of cultivating a sense of neurodivergent athletes' membership on her team through visibility and demonstrating care. However, members of minoritized communities should not bear the burden of challenging and changing exclusionary norms and structures, as athlete Nicole had to in the example shared above. The coactive process requires the involvement of *all* team members. People who are not members of minoritized communities must also take action to disrupt and prevent exclusion. The coaches in this chapter discuss how they aim to demonstrate care and support for team members and to learn from them about who they are. When team members demonstrate care, they can recognize and celebrate their differences and support one another in the ways each person needs.

Asian American studies and disability studies scholar Dr. Mimi Khúc sheds light on how a person's unwellness arises from living within "structures of unwellness" (Khúc, 2023, p. 5) (e.g., racism, ableism). In Khúc's (2023) conversations with Asian American college students about the meaning of mental health, they discussed:

> Feeling safe. Belonging. Having community that you trust. Liking yourself. Experiencing a full range of feelings, not numbness. Feeling fulfilled. Having a purpose. Healthy boundaries. A supportive community. Feeling valued. Feeling understood. The ability to 'be yourself.' Hope. Feeling like you have a future. Being happy. Laughing. Being able to be vulnerable with others. Holding loved ones. Agency—feeling like you have control and can make choices.
>
> (p. 32)

These responses highlight the *felt* internal and social experiences associated with mental health. None of these ideas refer to winning or accomplishments, in alignment with Polyvagal Theory, which stresses that a person's nervous system must *feel* safe with others to develop a sense of community. In other words, the well-being of each "I" is required to build a team and is also continuously impacted by interactions with team members. It is important to name here that Polyvagal Theory arose from psychology, the field that Khúc critiques due to its history of classifying experiences and behaviors emerging from structures of unwellness as medical conditions. Khúc explains, "we need to move away from the medical model of individual pathology toward a model focusing on larger structures of unwellness" (Khúc, 2023, p. 5).

If we embrace Khúc's call to view social structures as the source of unwellness rather than an individual problem, we can use Polyvagal Theory as a tool for making sense of how the social systems we navigate impact our well-being.[1] We can then work to change the harmful systems. Data from the U.S. Center for SafeSport demonstrates the relationship between experiences of harm and mental health challenges. For example, athletes reported that "unwanted sexual experiences [in the context of their sport involvement] resulted in athletes' perceptions of themselves being negatively impacted, followed by adverse mental health outcomes" (U.S. Center for SafeSport, 2024, p. 57). Through the lens of Polyvagal Theory, we can view poor mental health as a response to an environment in which people feel unsafe and seek to understand why, as Khúc encourages us to do. With this in mind, as coactors, we can embrace our responsibility for contributing to an environment where others feel safe. Different people have different needs to feel safe due to their unique experiences. So, it is vital to recognize each of the "I"s on our team. Coaction also requires us to pay attention to our interconnectedness. A team forms through the mutually supportive relationships among the "I"s.

A culture of mutual support might look like this:

- When teaching others, trying different methods to best fit the needs of the learner, as Jackie's mom modeled.
- Coach Johnson-Crowder expressing her own needs to the team, modeling that asking for support is okay, and athletes responding by expressing their own needs and supporting Coach Johnson-Crowder and their teammates.
- Coach Feldman trusting athletes to know when they need flexibility and time for themselves for their well-being and responding with support. He does not question whether their request is valid or their commitment to the team. Rather, he views accommodating individual needs as demonstrating that he values every team member.

In these examples, team members demonstrate that they recognize others will have unique needs, seek to understand them, and strive to support their team members as they work together.

Lift Up Others' Voices

A coach's lived experiences will not always mirror those of their athletes. Fortunately, sameness is not required for a coach to cultivate a culture of mutual support. Athletes say a coach's or athlete's gender does not determine effective coaching. Instead, athletes prefer coaching styles that any coach, regardless of gender identity, could demonstrate (Hovden & Tjønndal, 2019). Coaches can strive to get to know athletes as whole, complex people and tailor their coaching behaviors to meet their unique needs.

Men have been and continue to be favored for leadership positions in college sport (National Collegiate Athletic Association, 2024). Some athletes and coaches may assume that women will coach with a feminine style ineffective for men (presumably masculine) athletes (Hovden & Tjønndal, 2019; Walker & Bopp, 2011), whereas men are perceived as capable of coaching men and women athletes (Kalin & Waldron, 2015). However, athletes' preference for men may be due to a lack of experience with women coaches (Kalin & Waldon, 2015), suggesting that athletes' perspectives may change if more women were present in coaching roles.

Nicole's story indicates that coaches' gender identities may influence how they coach. We shouldn't assume that a coach will have certain beliefs or employ a particular style because of their gender identity. Instead, as Batliwala (2011) indicates, we can acknowledge that past experiences are a part of the Self. Women coaches' behaviors may be informed by their own experiences of being underestimated or excluded in sport, which has historically privileged men and qualities associated with masculinity (Hovden & Tjønndal, 2019; Sullivan Barak et al., 2021; Walker & Sartore-Baldwin, 2013). However, coaches may have had varied experiences even if they share a gender identity. Regardless of gender identity, all coaches can reflect on their empowering and problematic experiences as athletes and strive to apply what they have learned to enable athletes to use their power.

As a coach, you do not have to conform to a particular coaching style due to your gender or other identities. Adopting a flexible approach requires us to resist assuming a woman or a feminized style of coaching would be most effective for women athletes. Instead, you can choose a coaching style that you believe most authentically demonstrates who you are and will best support your athletes. As the coaches in this chapter model, you can meet each athlete where they are, learn about their goals, needs, experiences, and identities, and adapt your coaching accordingly. This requires you to be flexible with your coaching style; people change over time, and therefore, the way you can best support an athlete may also change. Different athletes will also respond differently to your coaching.

Coaches can also highlight stories of other role models who are different from themselves but to whom athletes can relate. Kenza's story highlights how role models she could relate to, whom she didn't know personally, shaped her athletic aspirations. Dr. Sara Ahmed's (2017) term "citational relational" refers to the idea that people cite people they are familiar with; this creates a chain reaction in which a select few people become recognized as experts within a social circle as people continue to cite them. Ahmed explains that repeatedly citing people who share the same identities and perspectives builds a metaphorical wall, excluding people who do not share the identities and perspectives of those cited.

Sharing stories of role models with varied identities and experiences creates a broader citational web of references. When coaches repeatedly share examples of role models with the same identities and qualities, this tells athletes there is a specific way they must identify or act. If an athlete does not see people they relate to through shared identities among their coaches or the role models that coaches introduce them to, this absence becomes a barrier to seeing the team as a welcoming space. It may also be difficult for an athlete to imagine possibilities for themselves within sport if they don't see others like them. A coach who provides examples of diverse role models who engage in coaction enables athletes to see people like themselves as leaders and opens the door to athletes imagining who can be a coactor and how they can engage in coaction.

As discussed in Chapter 2, the difference between someone who engages in coaction and someone who does not is not their ability. It is believing they have valuable assets and opportunities on the team. It is hearing they have skills that contribute to the team's work. It is seeing people like themselves, including those with identities, personalities, skills, and experiences, engaging in coaction and being recognized by others as capable coactors. It is having a chance to try new skills and responsibilities and the flexibility to make mistakes rather than fear failure. It is collaborating to share responsibilities rather than proving one's independence through a solo trial.

With this understanding of coaction in mind, it becomes clear that recognizing athletes' individuality and participation in coaction on their teams are intertwined. For an athlete to feel like they have valuable insights and skills to contribute to the team, coaches and teammates must cultivate a space where team members are affirmed and feel like they can express themselves. An athlete who feels valued is more likely to want to contribute. Team members must appreciate their teammates' diverse experiences and skill sets. Coaches can seek to learn about their athletes, the insights and skills they bring to the team, and the support they need. They can then find ways to enable athletes to contribute, bringing new strengths to the team rather than conforming to predetermined roles held by former teammates.

As stated at the beginning of this chapter, individuals form a team to pursue a shared purpose that they cannot achieve on their own. Recognizing the "I"s on the team is fundamental to working together effectively, from the moment they come together to determine their purpose. To define and achieve their purpose, team members must learn about one another's values, principles, strengths, and challenges. They must then determine how they can align their efforts to each contribute in a way that makes the most of their unique assets and needs. Learning from one another and finding alignment also requires expressing power with one another. The next chapter will guide you through how you can express power with team members.

Steps to Support Team Members as Their Full Selves

As coaches, we can cultivate a culture of mutual support on our teams in multiple ways.

1. Invite athletes to share their identities as they feel comfortable. Requiring athletes to disclose their identities is counterproductive; doing so can cause discomfort and undermine trust. If an athlete has not shared their identities with you, do not make assumptions about their identities or treat them differently based on your perceptions. Open the door with small, frequent opportunities. For example:
   a. Invite athletes to create playlists with their favorite music for the team to listen to during practice or team travel.
   b. Have a team cooking challenge in which team members share a dish that is important to them.
   c. Ask athletes what they look forward to during the week or about a highlight from the past week.

   Through small but frequent opportunities to express themselves, athletes can disclose information about themselves and have the flexibility to share to the extent that they are comfortable. Participate in these activities alongside athletes.
2. As previously discussed, we cannot expect athletes to feel comfortable sharing about themselves if we, their coaches, don't share anything personal. Furthermore, a coach should not expect athletes

to disclose anything they feel uncomfortable sharing. Coaches can set this example. Coaches are part of the team, and our participation fosters trust.

3 Check in with athletes about their feelings before diving into practice for the day. For example:
   a Ask each team member to share how they are feeling in one to three words. This enables you and the other athletes to be more aware of teammates' feelings. A base level of trust among athletes is required to ensure honest answers. You can cultivate trust by engaging in actions like those Coach Staley and Coach Feldman discussed.
   b Ask all team members to give a thumbs up, sideways thumb, or thumbs down, or hold up their fingers to show a rating of one to five to indicate how they feel. This is an efficient way to get a sense of the overall state of the team.

   A simple daily check-in demonstrates that you care about athletes for more than their athleticism. Taking the team's temperature can contribute to athletes' physical and mental development—knowing how athletes feel means you can adapt the practice as needed. If an athlete is exhausted when they arrive at practice, will a physically intense workout improve their skills and fitness, or will it dig them into a deeper hole of exhaustion? Similarly, if an athlete is stressed when they arrive at practice, will practicing technical or tactical skills that require focus be productive?

   In contrast, if an athlete feels energized, you can challenge the athlete a little more because you know they're prepared to handle it. You'll need to do some creative tailoring to account for all players' needs; do your best to account for extremes and address different players' situations throughout the week so each athlete receives individual attention.

4 Athletes seek role models to whom they can relate based on shared identities, experiences, and interests. Along with opening up about yourself, as discussed in recommendation one, provide examples of role models who have diverse identities. You can do this by:

   - Sharing articles, social media posts, podcasts, and books that feature diverse athletes.
   - Read, listen to, and discuss these materials with your team.

5 Explicitly discuss current social issues with your team. You do not have to be an expert on all social issues. You can:

   - Share educational articles, social media posts, podcasts, and books you found informative with your team and discuss them together.
   - Host guest speakers.
   - Involve athletes in educating the team by asking them to share educational resources, facilitate discussions, or request speakers they would like to invite.

Engaging in these activities with the team demonstrates the importance of creating a culture of mutual support. Cultivate this type of team culture by enabling athletes on your team to understand one another; learn about, recognize, and celebrate differences; and hold one another accountable for behaving with care and respect.

Reflection Questions

1 What opportunities do you provide for team members to discuss themselves and what they care about? Do you already engage in any of the suggested steps in the previous section? If not, what is one activity that seems manageable? When could you do this with your team?
2 What opportunities do you offer for team members to talk about what is happening in their lives outside of sport? If you have not already done this, when might you take time for personal check-ins with team members?
3 Do you discuss role models with your team? If so, who do you share as examples? Do you offer examples of role models with diverse identities and experiences? How might you expand the list to continue or start offering more diverse examples of role models?
4 Do you provide formal or informal educational opportunities for your team to discuss current social issues? What helpful educational resources could you share with your team? Who could you invite as a guest speaker to facilitate an educational discussion?

Note

1 If applied in this way, Polyvagal Theory is in alignment with the social model of disability as explained by Olkin (2022).

References

Ahmed, S. (2017). *Living a feminist life*. Duke University Press. https://doi.org/10.2307/j.ctv11g9836

Batliwala, S. (2011). *Feminist leadership for social transformation: Clearing the conceptual cloud*. Crea.

Glenn, E. N. (2011). Constructing citizenship: Exclusion, subordination, and resistance. American Sociological Review, 76(1), 1–24. doi:10.1177/0003122411398443

Greey, A. D. (2022). 'It's just safer when I don't go there': Trans people's locker room membership and participation in physical activity. *Journal of Homosexuality*, *70*(8), 1609–1631. https://doi.org/10.1080/00918369.2022.2038968

Hovden, J. & Tjønndal, A. (2019). The gendering of coaching from an athlete perspective: The case of Norwegian boxing. *International Review for the Sociology of Sport*, *54*(2), 239–255. https://doi.org/10.1177/1012690217715641

Kalin, J. L., & Waldron, J. J. (2015). Preferences toward gender of coach and perceptions of roles of basketball coaches. *International Journal of Exercise Science*, *8*(4), 303–317. https://digitalcommons.wku.edu/ijes/vol8/iss4/1/

Khúc, M. (2023). *dear elia: Letters from the Asian American Abyss*. Duke University Press.

LaVoi, N. M., & Dutove, J. K. (2012). Barriers and supports for female coaches: An ecological model. *Sports Coaching Review*, *1*(1), 17–37. http://dx.doi.org/10.1080/21640629.2012.695891

National Collegiate Athletic Association. (2024). *NCAA demographics database* [Data visualization dashboard]. NCAA. https://www.ncaa.org/about/resources/research/ncaa-demographics-database

Olkin, R. (2022). *Conceptualizing disability: Three models of disability*. American Psychological Association. https://www.apa.org/ed/precollege/psychology-teacher-network/introductory-psychology/disability-models

Staley, D. (2015, June 15). The secret. *The Players' Tribune*. https://www.theplayerstribune.com/articles/dawn-staley-south-carolina-coach

Sullivan Barak, K., Kaunert, C. A., Krane, V., & Ross, S. R. (2021). Divergent perspectives: Post-Title IX sportkids' views of female athletes, *Women in Sport and Physical Activity Journal*, *29*(2), 152–162. https://doi.org/10.1123/wspaj.2021-0024

U.S. Center For SafeSport. (2024). *2024 Athlete culture & climate survey report*. https://uscenterforsafesport.org/wp-content/uploads/2024/07/CultureClimateSurvey_ExternalReport_071824_v1.6.pdf

Walker, N. A., & Bopp, T. (2011). The underrepresentation of women in the male-dominated sport workplace: Perspective of female coaches. *Journal of Workplace Rights*, *15*(1), 47–64. http://dx.doi.org/10.2190/WR.15.1.d

Walker, N.A., & Sartore-Baldwin, M. L. (2013). Hegemonic masculinity and the institutionalized bias toward women in men's collegiate basketball: What do men think? *Journal of Sport Management*, *27*, 303–3015.

Yazeed, C. (2021, December 12). *The dangers of courage culture and why Brené Brown isn't for Black folk*. Dr. Carey Yazeed. https://drcareyyazeed.com/the-dangers-of-courage-culture-and-why-brene-brown-isnt-for-black-folk/

4 Share the Power

On sport teams, power is typically distributed among members through formal roles, ranked within a hierarchical structure. The head coach is at the top; below them are assistant coaches. Support staff members, like athletic trainers or sport psychologists, may be on the same level as or below the assistant coaches. The captains are on the next level, often serving as "middle managers" between the coaches and the other athletes. These different roles do not inherently come with power.

Instead, due to positional authority, the people in these leadership roles gain extrinsic power (Batliwala, 2011). Extrinsic power is not something a person possesses; rather, it exists within relationships with those willing to follow someone's guidance out of deference to their position. This deference may be based on respect or compliance. A formal leadership position also does not ensure that others are invested in the person as a leader. Expectations for what these roles—head coach, assistant coach, trainer, captain—entail and how people should relate to one another have been established through their acceptance and frequent application within sport culture.

As a coach, you have options for determining expectations for how team members work together. The traditional hierarchical leadership structure encourages these expectations to come from the top down; the person in a leadership role oversees others. So, logically, they would set expectations for those below them. However, as the coaches and athletes in this chapter explain, operating according to this hierarchical structure constrains team members' involvement and collaboration and poses risks to the team's stability. As discussed throughout this book, everyone on your team has power within. Chapter 2, "The New Framework: The Coactive Process," observes that, as coaches,

DOI: 10.4324/9781003605485-4

we cannot give athletes power; we enable them to express or prevent them from expressing their power. Athletes may not express their power because they view the coach as someone with power over them. Instead of attempting to give or withhold power, you can invite team members to share how they believe team members should act and collaboratively set expectations informed by their perspectives. Team members can learn about one another and co-create expectations, encouraging each person to express their whole selves and apply their strengths without fear of judgment. In this model of power, all team members, including coaches and athletes, can express power with one another. Throughout this chapter, coaches and athletes describe why and how expressing power with one another supports individual team members and the whole team.

As discussed in Chapter 2, self-motivation arises from a sense of competence, autonomy, and relatedness. If you want all team members to be motivated to actively contribute to the team, it is important for you and other team members to affirm their ability to do so and provide opportunities. Relegating an athlete to "follower" undermines this possibility. Additionally, Polyvagal Theory indicates that a sense of safety facilitates social connection, another key to effective collaboration among team members. Requiring athletes to defer to people in leadership roles, including some of their teammates, creates a division among team members and may form a threat environment in which they must demonstrate to leaders that they are a good follower, or prove they can lead. Athletes in leadership roles may also experience a threat environment, because they must prove that they can maintain their status. How might this undermine team members' ability to build supportive relationships?

Listening, Seeing, and Learning

Expressing power with one another is fundamental to building relationships. In an interview, Coach Staley explained why building relationships with athletes is important to her, and how she does it.

> I know people. I know my separation in coaching has a lot to do with my interaction and me forging relationships with people so that's what I'm going to expound on. The X-ing and O-ing? It's X-ing and O-ing. You can learn that. I think I have things that coaches can't learn at this point of their careers because it is the very thing

> that I've built my career on, which is the person and figuring out how to deal with them and all the things that they're thinking about and all the things that they want to achieve while not compromising the sanctity of the team.
>
> You have to forge that relationship with each and every player. You have to manage that, and again, I go back to my point guard skills. I know I'm the coach. I know I'm the coach. They know they're the superstars. They know they're the role players so what I would do is it's just communicating. It's frank conversations. You'll figure out how they like to take in information because ultimately you want them to be who they are while respecting the whole sanctity of the team.
>
> (Gervais, 2021, para. 13–14)

Staley (2023) also described why communication is an important part of coach-athlete relationships:

> The best way to be able to help them is to allow them to be heard. I think coaches have a tendency to just talk and talk and talk and talk and you don't really know if your message is being heard. You know you are delivering it, but you don't really know if your message is being heard. The basketball part of it takes place on the court, but taking a vested interest outside of basketball really allows me to have more of an impact on the court.
>
> (para. 9)

Coach Staley's discussion of listening to athletes and individualizing her communication with them shows how a coach and athletes can share power with one another. By expressing power with athletes in this way, she also demonstrates her care for team members as complex people. As discussed in Chapter 3, she recognizes and shows that she values the unique self each person brings to the team.

In addition to responding to each athlete's individuality, Coach Staley celebrates their contributions by publicly recognizing all team members. Following a national championship win in 2022, Coach Staley said,

> I have to give a real good shout-out to the players who don't get into the game a lot. We have 16 players, and a lot of them, probably seven or eight, who prepared us for UConn, prepared us for

> Louisville, prepared us for Creighton, never got to shine. So, I'm going to give them a shine right now.

Then Coach Staley named every player on her team (Yeager, 2022, para. 5), publicly disrupting the hierarchical division between players on the court and those on the sidelines. While some athletes had the opportunity to demonstrate their skills in front of fans and directly contribute to gameplay, Coach Staley highlighted that every team member's contributions throughout the process of working together enabled the team to win.

Yoga instructor Nikki also spoke about attempting to challenge and subvert traditional hierarchies in yoga, which can be applied to other physical activities and sport teams.

> I've always been really into team sports. I liked being like a captain of the team and being in a minimal leadership role. I think yoga teaching lends itself to that. We're always striving in the practice of yoga to dismantle hierarchies. Yoga has classically been quite hierarchical throughout history, which has caused a lot of issues. In modern-day yoga, it is important for us to be really conscious of the history and to recognize how to move beyond that model so that you don't end up with power imbalances and all of the issues that have existed since the beginning when there was this really differentiated teacher and student dynamic. The student was dependent on the teacher.

Nikki elaborated on one way that someone in a formal leadership role, such as a teacher, studio owner, or coach, can disrupt the power imbalance between themselves and students or team members. Her explanation highlights the risk of depending on one or a few leaders to support a team and how engaging in coaction may create more stable and supportive conditions for team members.

> To be a good leader, you have to know when it's time to get help. Know what your weaknesses are and what your strengths are and don't feel that you have to do everything, because if you're not good at things and you're trying to do them anyway, you can get into trouble. I think it requires a certain amount of surrender to the reality of who you are and if you can develop skills if you want to. You might not have the capacity to develop certain skills, but

maybe somebody else in your life has that skill, and they can fill that void or create an environment where you can lead in the ways that you are skilled and that you can step back in areas where you're not, and that prevents you from doing damage or being ineffective.

No one can be good at everything. Expecting a person in leadership to know what is best for everyone or to have all of the skills required to guide a team places an unrealistic and potentially harmful burden on them. Coach Staley and Nikki point out that all team members' contributions are valuable and necessary. If the coactive team is a braid of ropes, every team member's threads in the ropes make the braid stronger. Each offers strengths to the whole, and no one can contribute to the whole in the exact same way. Athletes have also noted that this is how they choose to practice leadership informally, even when a formal leadership hierarchy is imposed.

Athletes' Perspectives on Expressing Power with Teammates

While researching college athletes' understandings of leadership, I interviewed several college athletes about their viewpoints on team captains. Similar to Coach Staley and Nikki, these athletes discussed the risk of relying on leaders and the benefits of team members contributing unique strengths to their team. The following dialogue highlights common ideas from the discussion, like several team members leading in their own way, asking for support, and how team members feel when they have the opportunity to contribute.

Sonya: When you have one person telling everyone what to do, everyone else becomes followers. They don't become leaders themselves; they just do whatever the person says. They may not care about what they're doing because they're just doing what they're told. Cara: We have two captains. One is hurt, but she's basically a coach for us. When we go to the locker room at halftime, everyone listens to what she says because she's so smart about basketball. Everyone values her opinions. So, at that instance, everyone becomes her follower.

I think I'm a huge leader on the court. I calm people down in our huddles and I tell people the next play like, "Reset, it's ok, calm down. We're gonna do this on offense, that on defense." Everyone follows what I say in the huddles.

The other captain is the leader who reassures you and she also will make big plays for us, so she leads by both action and vocally. Then, my other teammate, I look up to her more as a leader during practice. Even though she doesn't play much in games, she plays so hard at practice. She makes everyone better, and I think that if people really believed and followed her doing that then we would be so competitive all the time at practice. That's not always the case. So, I think at different times all of us all of us step up as leaders. We all work together.

Tori: I [also] don't think the captain has to be the one leader because that can be an intimidating role to be put in. It's "all eyes on me" all of a sudden. It can be difficult at the beginning because everybody sees them as the go-to person, and the captain doesn't know every answer, or they might not know everybody yet. So, I think seeking help as a captain is perfectly fine, too, and encouraging others to help you lead so you're not all alone.

Sasha: I enjoy being a leader within the group because I don't need to be glorified. There's always a push to be a captain or, you know, be in leadership. I'm in leadership, I'm in SAAC [Student-Athlete Advisory Committee], I'm involved in a lot of other things, but those are not just one person being the star.

Erica: I think that, for our team in particular, we all just get along so well. We all motivate each other, so the captain role doesn't really come into play on a day-to-day basis. It's just when coach needs something done, he'll ask the captains, or if we have to have that hard conversation with someone it comes down to the captains. Like coach says, everyone has a role in leadership; it's not just the captains.

Molly: My freshman year, the team did a good job making the freshmen feel like we weren't freshmen and more like a teammate who can contribute. So, I've always kept that in mind. That's how I want the next people to feel because that's how I felt.

Fiona: I look up to every single person on our team for one thing or another. I don't think anyone's more of a leader than the other. I think the dynamic that we have is pretty good of people not being afraid to step in and lead or give ideas or lead by example when other people aren't.

Bailey: In high school, I didn't really have a team; it was kinda just me doing my own thing. Coming into this team, I wasn't sure how it would go, fitting in, but we're each our own type of leader and we're all just working towards being our best selves. Some people are more encouraging and vocal, and there's also some quiet ones, but they're still making an impact. So, everyone can be a leader; it's just they have different styles. Overall, we all want to accomplish stuff together and we care about each other a lot.

Erica: Yeah, we all know what to do. We don't have to have one person telling us what to do like you might think a captain would. At first, we did because we just didn't know the routine, but now we know, so we just go. I think everyone works together to have a good practice instead of just one person telling them what to do.

The athletes describe team dynamics, indicating that they neither want nor abide by a division between team members with or without formal leadership roles. They recognize that team members contribute to shared efforts in different, complementary ways. However, these athletes work together within a context in which leadership is prioritized; they do not have the terminology of coaction to describe how they work with their teammates.

How might teaching about and practicing coaction support their inclinations to collaborate with one another and enhance their ability to do so? How might this also encourage athletes who are hesitant to embrace leadership roles to engage more actively with team members?

Sharing Power through Team Structure

Safe, supportive relationships are fundamental to engaging in coaction (Porges, 1995, 2022). Creating a safe environment and providing meaningful support are both dependent upon shared power; a person who wants to provide safety and support must learn from the other person what they need to feel safe and supported (Haber et al., 2007). When team members feel seen, heard, valued, and are invited to be a coactor, they are more likely to want to continue to be a coactor (Deci

& Ryan, 1985). The braid-like dynamic of a coactive team enables relationship-building and collaboration, and all members of a coactive team contribute to the process of working together. Unlike the traditional pyramidal, hierarchical leadership structure, there are no ranks. No team member or their contributions are valued over others. Every team member is valuable as they are, has strengths they can contribute now, and has room to grow.

The traditional hierarchical leadership structure applied in sport to distribute extrinsic power among team members is consistent with leadership structures in other organizational contexts. For example, an executive director of an organization is expected to oversee directors, who oversee assistant directors, and so on. This structure serves a functional purpose. By defining roles and who has power over whom, organization members have a clearer sense of how specific responsibilities are allocated and to whom they report.

One might expect that this enables efficiency within an organization. However, research demonstrates that an imposed leadership structure does not ensure effective leadership, nor do team members necessarily view those in formal leadership positions as effective (Fransen et al., 2014, 2015). As the athletes who contributed to the dialogue suggest, they have expectations for how team members should engage with one another—regardless of the formal team leadership structure.

Leaving athletes' relationships to develop without intentional dialogue and focusing on a formal, hierarchical leadership structure is an investment in a compliance-based team culture. Prioritizing leadership development implies that if a few team members are sufficiently capable of performing leadership as the coach has prescribed, other team members will follow their guidance. However, every athlete can think for themselves; they have power within. They may comply, but this is not an indication of satisfaction, and it does not encourage team members who are "followers" by default to contribute in their own ways. Some team members subvert imposed expectations and establish their own. In contrast, if you express power with team members, such as in the ways Coach Staley and Nikki describe, you can collaboratively determine expectations for coaction so everyone has a shared, inclusive understanding of how they can work together.

From a person-centered perspective, consider that someone's experience within an organization will impact their overall well-being. If only a select few people on the team are designated leaders, many people won't receive recognition for their contributions. Insisting on a hierarchical leadership structure willfully ignores the importance of the contributions of "lower-ranking" individuals to the success of those in superior positions. Formal leaders receive recognition and validation for their own efforts and the team's success. Applying formulaic expectations for a leader's role also constrains what contributions are worth recognizing and can change how they contribute. Consequently, some of the strengths that a person in a leadership role has may be overlooked.

For those not recognized as leaders and those who are, these limitations affect the possibility of fulfilling each individual's three psychological needs: competence, autonomy, and relatedness. As discussed in Chapter 2, the fulfillment of psychological needs contributes to intrinsic motivation. If an athlete does not experience a sense of competence, autonomy, and relatedness, their investment in actively contributing to team efforts will suffer. Several studies show that fulfillment of psychological needs is associated with well-being (Reis et al., 2000; Thomaes et al., 2017)—and if an athlete is not well, they will not perform at optimal capacity.

Sonya's comment in the dialogue above highlights another reason traditional leadership structures can limit team members' engagement, especially if they are not captains. When one leader expresses power over team members, team members are not encouraged to think for themselves or contribute their ideas. This exemplifies the concept of docile bodies (Foucault,1995).

When a person is a docile body, they are passive and compliant. They have learned or been required to follow externally imposed rules and expectations. In a hierarchical team structure, "followers" comply with instructions given by higher-ranking team members or coaches. They learn that a "good" team member mirrors what others do, leading to a culture of conformity.

In such a culture, athletes are taught to not use their power within. Instead, they learn to allow others to express power over them. Offering their own insights and ideas may be perceived as disruptive; the athlete who asserts themselves and expresses dissent becomes a problem. In contrast, assertiveness from leaders is praised. Followers learn to emulate leaders if they want to express their ideas. However, even if they become a formal leader, they will not have practice sharing their ideas. Innovation will be difficult because they have not had to think for themselves, nor have they had the opportunity to have their original ideas affirmed by others. In a hierarchal team structure, athletes give up their power to be "coachable" in sport, learning expectations for themselves and others that impact how they express power in other contexts.

Based on traditional leadership practices in sport, we often treat exceptional compliance with team norms as leadership. In contrast, we treat striving to lead differently as disruptive because it requires questioning and experimentation. If athletes feel speaking their minds and asking questions will result in others labeling them disruptive or incapable of leadership, their ability to develop the skills needed to work effectively with others is limited. Compliance is the opposite of collaboration. If we, as coaches, prepare athletes to apply their skills outside of sport, focusing on leadership development hinders these efforts, too. Why would an athlete believe they should be assertive in work, school, or other settings if they associate sport leadership with compliance, a context that is central to their lives and sometimes even their identity? Athletes in leadership roles may be assertive and feel rewarded for their assertiveness. However, in the dialogue above, athletes indicate they are uncomfortable being put on the spot. They expect a leader to have all the answers. They view a leader as superior to others and someone who may crave external recognition.

The dialogue sheds light on how the traditional conceptualization of leadership in sport limits athletes' participation. As noted earlier in this chapter, if leadership is hierarchical, directions should come from the top; leaders should express their power over their followers. Logically, a leader would not consult with other team members as equals; admitting they need help may threaten their status. The leader, whether coach or captain, may not have the same concerns or needs as the team members, nor will they know everything about every team member. The tools and ideas they may consider to address an issue will be limited to those they possess. If a leader makes a decision based on their perspective alone, they may inadvertently thwart other team members' needs. If one person leads the group, all followers will look to the leader for directions.

No one person has all the answers. Even if they have an answer, it is just one way of responding. As a coach, your perspective is limited by your own experience. The same is true for athletes. You and athletes may overlook valuable insights if you don't consult with others. Making a decision without consulting with others may also put others at risk; an individual may not be aware of how their decision will impact others if they do not ask for their input.

Reflecting on the constraints a hierarchical leadership structure imposes on athlete engagement raises crucial questions.

- At what point should an athlete switch gears from being a good follower to striving to be a leader?
- What differentiates team members' perception of viewing specific behaviors as leadership versus being a troublemaker disrupting team norms?

Coaction offers an equitable approach to collaboration that does not require team members to accept a follower status or earn a leadership status. Several aspects of engaging in coaction also facilitate team members' self-motivation to actively contribute to team efforts. Coaction enables team members to embrace their own and others' current strengths. In doing so, team members support one another's sense of competence and relatedness. Coaction enables recognition of areas for growth as part of being human; every team member can continue to learn and develop their strengths. Varied strengths and growth opportunities enable team members to identify how to make the most of complementary contributions. Choosing how they want to contribute and deciding with teammates how they will work together supports team members' sense of autonomy. When team members recognize and value differences, questions and disagreements are expected rather than disruptive. Collaborating and working through questions and disagreements enable athletes to learn from one another; every member can be both a teacher and a learner. This also supports all three psychological needs, because athletes are able to actively contribute to working through conflicts, not comply with imposed decisions made by a select few.

Enabling Athletes to Use Their Power

Does a hierarchical leadership structure feel familiar to you? Perhaps you experienced it as an athlete. Maybe it sounds like the team you currently coach. Why is this the team structure that teams so frequently adopt? Many coaches are former or current athletes, and our past experiences inform our everyday decisions. If an athlete becomes a coach, how they were coached likely enabled them to succeed and motivated them to pursue a career in sport. However, as discussed in previous chapters, many people are excluded from participating in sport. If we continuously coach as we were coached, we are more likely to cater to athletes who "fit into" the status quo, upholding exclusionary sport culture and traditional approaches to leadership.

But it doesn't have to be this way. You can adapt your coaching to fit the unique individuals on your team. You can better support all your athletes by learning from them and integrating their ideas into your coaching behaviors and expectations. Recall that a person's power within is expressed through their ability to think for themselves. Communication is how knowledge, and therefore power, is shared. Coach Staley highlighted this when she discussed the importance of allowing athletes to be heard. The athletes who participated in the dialogue also recognized that they could express power with their teammates because they experienced the benefits of different teammates' contributions. However, they provided examples of leaders expressing power with and over one another, reflecting their investment in their relationships while operating within a traditional leadership structure.

As a coach, expressing power with the team members by inviting them to share their insights means everyone can learn with and from one another. Expressing power with others means exploring the question in-depth and arriving at an answer that accounts for multiple perspectives, and possibly additional questions to explore. Responsibility for supporting team members is distributed, removing the pressure for the leader to be "the knower." Sharing power also elevates other team members' knowledge. In a hierarchical leadership structure, followers are viewed as inferior. When team members are coactors, they can explore questions as equally valuable knowers. Depending on the topic at hand, some team members may have more expertise than others, but this does not confer superior status.

Proactively set up structures and model behaviors encouraging team members to express power with one another. The stories above indicate that sharing power with others can positively impact individuals' well-being, interpersonal relationships, and athletic performance. Coach Staley and Nikki aim to share power with athletes, colleagues, and students. The college athletes I spoke with indicated that their teammates express power with one another by demonstrating that they value each person and encourage them to contribute their unique skills.

Coaction Depends on Relationships, Not Titles

You can create opportunities for the athletes you coach to express their power with one another by fully engaging them in the coactive process. As team members work through the coactive process, together, everyone can determine the team's purpose, identify alignment and determine how to navigate differences among team members' values and principles, and create shared expectations about everyday practices that team members will demonstrate to contribute to the achievement of their shared purpose. This process will require ongoing dialogue and consensus-building. Chapter 5, "Co-Creating Purpose," and Chapter 6, "Building a Foundation through Alignment, Not Sameness," will expand on how to work through this coactive process. For now, we will focus on the influence of team structure on athletes' abilities to express their power.

In the dialogue, athletes said they see multiple team members as leaders, and the leader varies depending on the context and team members' needs. What is the point of assigning formal leaders if athletes look to other team members for support? How might assigning leadership roles impact the rest of the team's self-confidence, self-efficacy, and leadership development?

Imagine restructuring a hierarchical team structure in which a few team leaders are positioned as leaders above their followers, and followers are expected to aspire to climb the ladder to become leaders. As explained in Chapter 2, "The New Framework: The Coactive Process," coaction offers an alternative braid-like structure. Team members do not hold ranks. Instead, they are each an invaluable thread in the braided ropes interconnected with team members; they are coactors. Each member has a role co-determined with other team members, and no role is more important than another. Just like each thread in a rope, every team member's contributions, in any role, make the team stronger. Positions are not permanent; threads in a braid shift their position in relation to one another throughout the braid. Coactors take turns, as discussed in the strategies in the next section.

If your team takes this approach to fulfilling responsibilities, each team member's contributions are recognized as important for the team's collective well-being and success. A braid is dynamic; it can stretch, shift, expand, and reshape according to the team's needs, interests, and goals. When your team members don't have statuses that indicate who's in charge and who's expected to comply, they can experiment with new ways of working together. For example, one especially observant team member may be the hype person, who prioritizes noting what team members are doing well during practice, and calling out what they notice in the moment with a phrase or cheer the team creates. Another team member who is an attentive listener may take on the role of conflict transformation facilitator, who gathers perspectives on team conflicts and then facilitates a conversation to address it.[1] Overtime, other team members may be interested in taking on these roles and collaborate with team members who currently hold them (all team members can become hype people), or one team member may change their role and hand it off to another teammate.

This idea may raise concerns for you. Where do you stand within this braid as a coach? Doesn't this undermine your authority? A coach should not depend upon their status to earn athletes' respect. Relying on a higher-status position for respect is a form of expressing power over others. The coach-athlete relationship is what drives a coach's effectiveness. Aligned with Coach Staley's discussion of the coach-athlete relationship, sport leadership researcher Dr. Sophia Jowett (2017) states,

> When the quality of the relationship is good, coaching benefits because the relationship contains active ingredients (e.g., respect, trust, commitment, collaboration) that are important for positive and mutual influence. However, when the quality of the relationship is poor, coaching suffers because the relationship is absent of active ingredients that allow the coaches and athletes to care for, commit to, and cooperate with one another.
>
> (p. 156)

Will an athlete trust a coach who expects compliance because they hold a higher-ranking position? Or do athletes trust a coach who engages in dialogue, actively listens to, considers, and responds to their needs and input? Some athletes perform well under pressure. But do you want the athletes on your team to work hard because they fear the consequences or because they are proud of themselves and your team? Research indicates that athletes' confidence, perceived competence, and collective efficacy are greater when coaches build supportive relationships by providing inspiration, motivation, and encouragement, engaging in effective communication, and being considerate of individual needs (Forlenza et al., 2018; Price & Weiss, 2013).

Strategies for Sharing Power

To express power with the athletes you coach, try viewing your role as that of a facilitator. A facilitator engages team members in dialogue and co-constructs knowledge with team members rather than telling them what to do or directing them.

1 Proactively plan time for dialogue among team members. Sport teams often have limited time to work together, which can create a sense of urgency around getting through discussions to focus on practicing sport-specific skills. However, even highly skilled athletes will struggle if team members don't work well together.

Schedule 5–10 minutes at the beginning of each team gathering (e.g., team meetings and practices) to identify discussion topics. As the coach, you may have subjects in mind—invite all athletes to add to the list. Determine, as a team, when you will talk about each topic and the amount of time needed. Next, determine if the issue is pressing and if it will benefit the team to discuss it before moving on to practice. Together, commit to meeting for a dialogue at the time and for the amount of time that the team has agreed upon.

Accounting for individual team members' needs and goals requires team members to prioritize deliberation over efficient decision-making (e.g., a team vote in which the majority wins). Proactively investing time in discussing team members' needs and goals will enable team members to effectively work together when training and competing. A complete discussion may require reducing the amount of time for practice. However, building trusting relationships and addressing concerns means the team will have more focused practices.

Decisions still need to be made in the moment, especially during competitions. Establishing a foundation of mutual understanding enables team members to make split-second decisions that benefit the team and that others will trust.

2 Rotate responsibilities. Most athletes are accustomed to looking to their coach and team captains for directions and answers. Rotating duties can help athletes recognize their own and others' knowledge and skills. Start by collaboratively creating a list of responsibilities that need to be fulfilled for the team to achieve their vision of success. Encourage imagination and creativity, and identify team members' strengths. Responsibilities could include tasks like leading the team warm-up, uplifting team energy when morale is low, or becoming a sounding board for team members facing a challenge, in or out of sport. Invite each team member to identify at

least one strength other than their athletic performance. Ask team members to share fellow team members' strengths. Then compile a list of responsibilities. Invite team members to volunteer. They may take on more than one responsibility if needed and if they feel that the amount of energy required is manageable. Consider what responsibilities may be missing.

After each week, plan with the team to determine which responsibilities will be required during the upcoming week and have different team members take on the duties. If the responsibility requires some experience or consistency, have an experienced athlete collaborate with someone less familiar with the responsibility. The experienced athlete can help the less experienced athlete become more comfortable, and the less experienced team member may provide new insights. Athletes expand their skill sets by taking on multiple responsibilities and practicing effective collaboration. Additionally, this approach distributes responsibilities among team members rather than placing the burden of leadership on the shoulders of a few.

3 Involve athletes in decision-making. The extent to which athletes are enabled to contribute to co-constructing knowledge depends on the types of decisions they are engaged in making. Captains are often responsible for logistical decisions, like dressing up for a team spirit day or starting components of their training routine during a practice session. Athletes need the opportunity to practice making more significant strategic decisions. Simply giving athletes the perception of control does not disrupt controlling coaching practices (Denison & Mills, 2014). For example, choosing when the team will begin a part of their usual training routine is a constrained choice. Enabling athletes to choose which stretches or other exercises they would like to complete as part of their warm-up gives them autonomy to decide what will help them prepare for their training session.

As a coach, your role is to create a plan for the team informed by your professional training and expertise. Once you have a plan, invite athletes to ask questions and provide suggestions. Athletes know their bodies best, and they each have a unique perspective informed by their own athletic experiences. Maintain evidence-based training principles for athletic development but adjust the timing according to the athletes' needs. For example, together, consider the timing and energy demands of the academic semester in conjunction with the progression of your sport's season. There are multiple approaches to practicing specific skills, and athletes may find some techniques more enjoyable than others. Collaboratively determine how you can maximize joy as part of your training.

4 Explain the why. As mentioned previously, athletes often expect to receive directions from coaches. However, part of expressing power with athletes is ensuring they understand why you are giving them specific instructions. A coach is expected to have expertise that enables them to make decisions for the team. However, sharing the rationale behind practice plans or competitive strategies with athletes enables them to connect your instructions to their team's purpose and goals.

   You can explain the why at various times, such as covering the overall season plan with the team at the first meeting or reviewing the rationale for a drill at the beginning of practice. When athletes understand how an action contributes to their goals and the team's purpose, they cease being docile bodies and become coactors. They are not simply doing what they are told for the sake of being coachable. Instead, they can develop a personal rationale for their actions.

   Explaining the why also opens the door to dialogue. If athletes are confused or disagree, they can ask questions to gain clarity or work through a disagreement. Athletes might also have suggestions that strengthen your ideas. You may need to set time aside for team dialogue. Taking the time to explain the why demonstrates that you want to share your knowledge for the athletes' development and that you respect their knowledge.

Reflection Questions

1 What power structures have you experienced as an athlete and/or coach? How did those structures influence your behavior?
2 What is your team's current power structure? Is it organized hierarchically? Can you think of opportunities to allow athletes to share power?
3 Do you designate time for the team to make plans, share concerns, and problem-solve together regularly? If not, when might you schedule team time so the team can discuss these topics in a timely manner?

4 Do you explain the rationale behind your instructions? When and how might you incorporate these explanations into your discussions with your team?
5 How often do you involve athletes in decision-making? What types of decisions do you typically ask athletes to make? Which decisions could you invite athletes to participate in?
6 What responsibilities do you typically assign to team captains? How might these responsibilities be distributed among more team members of the team during the season?

Note

1 Roles inspired by Desautels (2020).

References

Batliwala, S. (2011). *Feminist leadership for social transformation: Clearing the conceptual cloud*. Crea.

Deci, E. L., & Ryan, R. M. (1985). *Intrinsic motivation and self-determination in human behavior*. Plenum Press.

Denison, J., & Mills, J. P. (2014). Planning for distance running: coaching with Foucault. *Sports Coaching Review*, *3*(1), 1–16. https://doi.org/10.1080/21640629.2014.953005

Desautels, L. L. (2020). *Connections over compliance: Rewiring our perceptions of discipline*. Wyatt-MacKenzie Publishing.

Forlenza, S. T., Pierce, S., Vealey, R. S., & Mackersie, J. (2018). Coaching behaviors that enhance confidence in athletes and teams. International Sport Coaching Journal, 5(3), 205–212. https://doi.org/10.1123/iscj.2017-0040

Foucault, M. (1995). *Discipline & punish: The birth of the prison*. Vintage Books.

Fransen, K., Van Puyenbroeck, S., Loughead, T. M., Vanbeselaere, N., De Cuyper, B., Vande Broek, G., & Boen, F. (2015). Who takes the lead? Social network analysis as a pioneering tool to investigate shared leadership within sports teams. *Social Networks*, *43*, 28–38. https://doi.org/10.1016/j.socnet.2015.04.003

Gervais, M. (2021). Dawn Staley 286: Discipline and mental fortitude [Audio podcast transcript]. In *Finding Mastery with Dr. Michael Gervais*. Finding Mastery. https://findingmastery.com/podcasts/dawn-staley/

Haber, M. G., Cohen, J. L., Lucas, T., Baltes, B. B. (2007). The relationship between self-reported received and perceived social support: A meta-analytic review. *American Journal of Community Psychology*, *39*(1-2), 133–44. https://doi.org/10.1007/s10464-007-9100-9

Jowett, S. (2017). Coaching effectiveness: The coach-athlete relationship at its heart. *Current Opinions in Psychology*, *16*, 154–158. https://doi.org/10.1016/j.copsyc.2017.05.006

Porges, S. W. (1995). Orienting in a defensive world: Mammalian modifications of our evolutionary heritage. A Polyvagal Theory. *Psychophysiology, 32*(4), 301–18. https://doi.org/10.1111/j.1469-8986.1995.tb01213.x

Porges S. W. (2022). Polyvagal Theory: A science of safety. *Frontiers in Integrative Neuroscience*, *16*, 1–15. https://doi.org/10.3389/fnint.2022.871227

Price, M. S., & Weiss, M. R. (2013). Relationships among coach leadership, peer leadership, and adolescent athletes' psychosocial and team outcomes: A test of transformational leadership theory. *Journal of Applied Sport Psychology*, *25*(2), 265–279. http://dx.doi.org/10.1080/10413200.2012.725703

Reis, H. T., Sheldon, K. M., Gable, S. L., Roscoe, J., & Ryan, R. M. (2000). Daily well-being: The role of autonomy, competence, and relatedness. *Personality and Social Psychology Bulletin*, *26*(4), 419–435. https://doi.org/10.1177/0146167200266002

Staley, D. (2023, May 21). "Challenged Accepted" by Dawn Staley. *Rising Coaches*. https://risingcoaches.com/blog/challenge-accepted-by-dawn-staley

Thomaes, S., Sedikides, C., van den Bos, N., Hutteman, R., & Reijntjes, A. (2017). Happy to be "me?" Authenticity, psychological need satisfaction, and subjective well-being in adolescence. *Child development*, *88*(4), 1045–1056. https://doi.org/10.1111/cdev.12867

Yaeger, D. (2022, April 4). South Carolina coach Dawn Staley shines light on bench players. *Forbes*. https://www.forbes.com/sites/donyaeger/2022/04/04/south-carolina-coach-dawn-staley-shines-light-on-bench-players/?sh=406b2cfd7fe6

5 Co-Creating Purpose

Take a moment to reflect on a time you shared an experience, not to achieve a goal, but to be part of something with others. For example, have you attended a professional sporting event and felt a communal sense of elation as you watched your favorite team score, and jumped and cheered alongside hundreds of fellow fans? Have you attended a concert and felt joy arise from dancing to a favorite song, feeling the rhythm in your bones alongside hundreds of other people? Collective effervescence (Durkheim, 1912/1915; Pizzaro et al., 2022) occurs when we have a sense of interconnectedness through a shared experience with others.

We may not consider such shared experiences a team experience because they require minimal interaction with others and tend to be momentary. However, reflecting on these experiences can inform how we think about our team's purpose. Purpose is often goal-oriented, particularly in sport, as the coaches and athletes in this chapter describe, but many factors contribute to individual and team performance. You have learned in prior chapters that a sense of safety underlies well-being and collaboration. When team members are well and collaborate effectively, they're more likely to win.

Regardless of the team's win-loss record, what do you hope athletes experience when you are together? What do you hope they will take away from having been a member of your team, other than performance marks in team record books? What would you and team members prioritize if you described your purpose as what you aim to experience together? For example, members of a team may decide that their purpose is "Creating a community of challenge and fun to facilitate growth on and off the court."[1] This purpose is not

DOI: 10.4324/9781003605485-5

dependent upon the team's competitive performance. It is dependent upon all team members' intentional everyday interactions with one another, to create a sense of community, challenge one another, create fun experiences, and support one another's growth. If team members experience a sense of community, feel challenged, have fun, and grow athletically and personally, the outcome of performing well competitively is also likely.

In the following dialogue, college athletes explain that they perceive a leader as a guide to achieve a shared outcome. These athletes negotiate the emphasis on performance as the purpose of sport while also indicating that a leader is someone committed to supporting others and who is willing to challenge the status quo. They suggest that a leader is innovative, encouraging team members to work differently together than they may have in the past. These athletes' discussion indicates they seek a purpose like the example provided. However, while the actions and characteristics the athletes discuss indicate that leaders are responsive to the needs of team members, they are framed within the desired outcome of winning competitions. As you read the dialogue, consider how team members' experiences might shift if they co-created a purpose centered on what they want to experience together rather than a single outcome they aim to achieve.

Lily: Leadership all comes down to leading others towards a common goal.

Molly: [I agree,] if you lead without a purpose, you're gonna hit a dead end.

Sasha: The word "leadership" means that you are taking initiative to stand up for what you believe in and not being afraid of what other people think. Really just being different and standing out. A lot of leaders don't follow everyone else. You don't always want to go with the flow.

Cara: [Yeah,] as a leader, you always have to fight for what you believe in and fight for who you believe in.

Kate: [A leader is] someone who is ambitious…I think having high expectations and high hopes is huge. I don't know many leaders who didn't have high hopes or high expectations. Being a visionary is having the bravery and creativity in one's mindset to see the full potential of something. For me, this goes hand in hand with the idea of trusting the process. To be a visionary, you have to serve each season of your life faithfully, holding onto the vision that you have and working towards that "fullest potential" every day.

Fiona: [And motivated!] You have to want it, or else you can't convince anyone else to want it as much as you do. [Being] dedicated is another thing that goes along with that.

Sasha: Yeah, if there's no motivation to get better or to be the best, then why are you here, what are you doing?

Nicole: If you don't care about the sport, then you're not gonna care about being a leader on the team, you're just gonna be going through the motions. You're not gonna care about improving the team as a whole. If you're hurt, it's hard to stay positive and think that you're still playing a role, but you are. You'll make it through it. Sometimes it's hard to remember that. A lot of people lose their drive, and they think other things are more important. Even if you're not competing, it's important to help the team because we all have goals, and the only way the goals are gonna happen is if we all work together and make the team the best that we can be. If nobody's willing to be a leader and show that, then we're never going to be able to reach our full potential.

Ana: I think that to be a good leader, you have to be game-changing. Sometimes we have to just change it up to see what works.

Piper: We need new ideas that continue to build on our existing traditions. [On] our team, we have some awesome traditions, and we've struggled the last few years. That's just the reality. We're not where the program was five or 10 years ago. So, [we have to] continue to do new things to grow. Needing new ideas to build on traditions means you're not losing sight of tradition if you do new things, but you gotta do new things to get better. As a leader, you can help stimulate or introduce new ideas and new traditions and new things that maybe you haven't done in the past.

Audra: [Thinking about the whole team] is definitely something that you have to learn because coming into college gymnastics, you're used to just fighting for yourself. From preseason and going into the season is when we have the final lineups of who's actually competing and who's not. If you're not in the lineup, you have to be happy for the people who are because it really is all about the team. You can use that to help you work harder and not take it personally. You shouldn't be hoping your teammates fall because you want to be in instead of them. It is important to take your competitiveness and use it to help you push forward and push the people who are in lineups. It isn't just about you. You should be able to take a step back. If you're not chosen, somebody else is better, and that's better for the team. That's what you want to happen. So, teaching that is important, especially to the younger girls on the team who aren't used to that and don't know that yet. Sit them down and talk to them and let them know, "It's ok if you feel like this, but just know that you're here for a purpose bigger than yourself and it's about the team now, it's not about you."

Erica: Everyone has goals and dreams. I think by working hard to achieve my goals I can inspire others to want to work hard and achieve their goals, no matter what they are. I think just seeing the success that a leader has inspires others to want to be successful in their own way.

Maria: I think of one person who was on my team when I was a freshman in high school. She had no reason to help me as much as she did, but she picked me up and really guided me to enjoy the sport and get really excited about it. You want to be powerful in a good way. Sometimes that word can come off as not the best because there's some people who are really powerful, but not in a very positive way. It's important to have a powerful impact on people that will help them rise to the occasion and just be better people. I wouldn't say there needs to be one powerful leader, but the team should be a powerful force.

These athletes explain that being a part of a team enables them to achieve more than they could on their own. Some are inspired by the support they have received and the challenges they have experienced. They indicate that, together, team members continuously strive for improvement. To "lead" suggests forward motion, aligned with continuous striving to win in sport.

In contrast to these athletes, yoga instructor Nikki pointed out the limitations of prioritizing continuous striving for individual and shared performance goals. Nikki proposed an alternative way of thinking about purpose, which yoga instructor and personal trainer KC built upon.

Nikki explained,

> In team culture, you're always told to do better, do better, do better, do better. Like runners, you know, you're literally being timed. It's super objective, "Okay, you did worse, or you did better, or you're doing the same." But you're supposed to be doing better. [In yoga,] there's no clock, … there's less measurement than what you would have ever experienced as a runner. It was mind-blowing to me. I still remember when they'd be like, "You look great, good job, amazing!" because you just don't hear stuff like that.
>
> My dad, he was pretty supportive [as a running coach], but it's still so rigorous. "This is what you can improve," and "The next time, you're going to fix this." There might be a fleeting moment where you did amazing, and you can ride that high for a hot second. But then you're just looking for a way to immediately supersede that.
>
> And so, there's very little satisfaction and contentment, I think, in sports in general, because even if you literally win, immediately, people are like, "Well, how can we do better next time?" Or they're already talking about next year. So, to do something that was not focused on destination or winning was very odd to me, and amazing.

KC added,

> In yoga there's something called dharma, which is similar to purpose. It's what you're meant to do. It's your mission. I like it because you can carry out your dharma throughout your life, but it doesn't need to look the same in all of the different phases, and it's not so fixed. So, I like looking at purpose this way, or maybe subbing in dharma for purpose, because I truly believe that we don't have to have a purpose. We're here to experience what it's like to be a human being, and just being a human being is a lot to go through. And it's beautiful, and even if you're just being a human being and you "don't accomplish anything" you're still beautiful, your life is still of value, and you're still doing it right.

Now, reconsider the athletes' dialogue. You may even read it again, keeping Nikki and KC's explanations of purpose in mind. Can a person in a leadership role fully support the holistic well-being of every team member if the team's purpose is to always strive to be better than before? What might athletes miss out on if they are always focused on proving their commitment to achieving their potential? How might they work differently together, and what might they gain from their athletic experience, if they focused on the experience they want to share? Winning can still occur, but what if their win-loss record didn't determine whether the team achieved their purpose?

Coaction allows team members to just be together, now. Reflection and rest are essential components of growth. These are actions that coactors can do with and alongside one another. Growth also does not always occur in a forward direction; sometimes, it requires stepping back. Coaction allows the team members' experiences to take the form and direction they need.

Keep in mind that the choice to engage in coaction requires a willingness to challenge traditional expectations of how teams work together: guided by a leader. Identifying a team purpose that is focused on co-creating an experience, not on achieving outcomes, is also likely to be an ideological and behavioral shift within a college athletic department. To determine how team members can co-create the experience they envision and to proactively address the challenges they may face in doing so, they must consider what is occurring around them.

Accounting for Context

The team's political context will inform its purpose. In the case of NCAA athletics, for example, the context includes NCAA policies, college policies, athletic department policies, team policies, and, for some athletic programs, state policies. The political context also includes informal expectations, like common ways of thinking about leadership and the purpose of sport within NCAA Division I college sport.

Currently, a meritocratic and hierarchical conceptualization of leadership is favored (Pape, 2019; Suyemoto & Ballou, 2007). The college athletes I interviewed are keenly aware that the purpose of NCAA Division I sport is to win competitions. Prioritizing competition encourages an understanding of leadership consistent with the traditional conceptualization of leadership by fostering a merit-based hierarchy. The athletes are aware of the pressure to win that comes with that hierarchy. Meanwhile, they also strive to create a more holistic purpose that supports their growth and well-being and that of their teammates. So, they must find ways to pursue this purpose within the constraints of the expectations imposed by their sport environment.

As you read at the beginning of this chapter, in my research with women in NCAA Division I athletics, many discussed envisioning possibilities and supporting teammates as their purposes. Their approach to these purposes included identifying personal competitive goals and cultivating team members' investment in their competitive purpose.

Many athletes indicated that a leader envisions possibilities for their team's purpose based on individual beliefs or power within. Some athletes also discussed leaders as change-makers. However, they also implied that the possibilities a leader envisions, or the change they are making, are focused on attaining higher levels of achievement.

Although the athletes discussed setting goals collaboratively to create buy-in, all team members are expected to be invested in competitive success; they are part of an NCAA Division I team. However, setting ambitious, competitive goals and defining success as achieving those goals do not account for the many ways athletes contribute to winning. Limiting the purpose of leadership to guiding the team through setting and achieving competitive goals overlooks the diverse assets everyone possesses.

Athletes recognized as leaders support their teammates not simply as athletes who score points but as whole people. Yet, only some team members are designated as team leaders. The athletes resist the idea that a leader's sole purpose is to guide the team to win. Instead, they believe that leaders develop supportive relationships with their teammates and cultivate enjoyment of playing their sport together. Building relationships enables team members to learn about each other's strengths and develop strategies for applying them, advancing their work together, and enjoying the process. Coactors treat competitive success as one of the outcomes of effectively working together rather than the purpose of being on the team.

Coaching within Traditional Sport Culture

Most coaches intend to support their athletes and enable them to think for themselves (Denison et al., 2017). However, policies at the government, NCAA, and department levels, NCAA expectations, and departmental influences affect coaches' positions within the hierarchy of collegiate athletics. In NCAA Division I athletics, a coach's success is often assessed by their wins, encouraging them to focus on competition. In this hierarchy, the coach also has positional authority (Batliwala, 2011). They can choose to express their power over the athletes and maintain the hierarchy or express power with them to cultivate a collaborative team structure (VeneKlasen & Miller, 2007). Denison and Mills encourage coaches to problematize practices that may "categorize, exclude, and regulate athletes" (Denison & Mills, 2014, p. 5). This includes problematizing what they do (and do not do) and say (and do not say) to athletes (Denison et al., 2017).

For example, suppose a coach directs athletes rather than asking for input. In that case, athletes do not receive the opportunity to enact change, or even to believe they could be capable of doing so. A coach can enable athletes to make decisions by providing choices and asking questions rather than giving directions. This approach shifts the power structure from a coach expressing power over athletes as their followers to expressing power with them as coactors.

As coaches, if we define the team's purpose for them, the available choices are constrained. For example, if we tell athletes that the team's purpose is to place third in the Conference Championship this season, this will guide their focus to making decisions that demonstrate their competitive drive. If the coach involves athletes in co-determining the team's purpose, instead, athletes can determine what they want to prioritize and why. By co-creating a team purpose, team members learn that their perspectives are valued in the most fundamental team decisions. If athletes believe that their shared experience is valuable because they have co-created this experience, and they feel that they are valued team members, this can contribute to achieving competitive outcomes without making competition the overriding focus.

Coach Johnson-Crowder, Coach Staley, and Coach Feldman offer expansive ways of thinking about athletes' purposes. All three coaches are invested in learning from athletes about what they want and need. When they discuss why and how they coach, they all emphasize their dedication to creating a fulfilling experience for athletes. In reflecting on the experiences she endured as an NCAA Division I athlete and professional athlete representing Jamaica, Coach Johnson-Crowder shared, "I was like, okay, either I am going to be destroyed by this, or I'm going to do something about it. So, I'm gonna coach…if you're gonna complain about something, at least try to do something to fix it. And that's what I did. I went into coaching."

When Coach Johnson-Crowder describes how she coaches, she demonstrates her investment in athletes' holistic well-being, something she did not experience as a collegiate and professional athlete.

> I let them know…our best bet at having you perform the way that we want you to perform is to give your mind, body, and spirit a chance to all be on one page and if one of them's not on the same page, we have to adjust. And that's okay. If the body is not on the same page, we're dialing down the workload because clearly… we're not trying to kill you. If the spirit's not aligned, then we might do some meditation through practice. We might do some meditation at the end of practice. We might start the practice that way. We might start the practice blind.
>
> So, for the throwers, they throw in a racquetball court, and when they do that, they can't see where the throws are going, because there's no reference for distance. So, if you're noticing that distance has been messing with your mind, and your experience is making you feel like, "Oh, I'm not doing enough." We're gonna throw in a racquetball court. I don't want you to see where it went because that stimulus is messing with you more than it's helping you. Sometimes it helps when you're at track meets. "Oh, that person threw further, I'ma get 'em." Cool. But sometimes it can put you in this chasing, chasing, chasing, chasing mentality where you can no longer focus on what you're actually doing.

College athletes want to compete well; high-performance levels are a rewarding aspect of sport. However, Coach Johnson-Crowder emphasizes that winning is not the focus; it occurs when a person is in alignment mentally, physically, and spiritually. In addition to focusing on individual well-being, Coach Johnson-Crowder views coaching as an opportunity to teach athletes about the relationship between self-awareness and collaboration.

> I tell [athletes] "Every judgment that you cast on others is a self-assessment you're not ready for yet." That sums up so much cause there's so much hurt and harm that we end up doing, unintentionally at times, simply because there's something about ourselves that we're not ready to tackle and we see in somebody else, so then we shame them for it.

Coach Johnson-Crowder teaches athletes to care for themselves and others. She does this through her words and actions. Her holistic approach benefits their athletic performance, but what they learn through their experience with her will extend beyond sport.

Coach Staley and Coach Feldman clearly state that they view their role and athletes' experiences on their team extending beyond sport. Both use the term "dream merchant" to describe their role as coaches. Coach Staley explained what being a dream merchant means to her.

> Anybody that is coaching this game, that's what you are. I know we try to figure out our purpose in coaching, and it's just that: being a dream merchant for young people. Helping young people find their passion [and] work towards that. It's not always basketball—it's not. For 90 percent of them, it's not basketball. It is figuring out what you want to do, because I want people to work in their passion. It is a lot easier to work in your passion if that's what you do on a daily basis. The real world really is taxing. It pulls you in a lot of different directions and if you're not passionate about it, you are not going to give it your full effort. And maybe half of you is good enough in some instances, but for you as a person, your fulfillment is most important.
>
> So, what does a dream merchant do? That person guides, that person helps to navigate, that person is a listener [and] an observer. That person is someone that is trustworthy of not only the student-athlete but everybody that touches that student-athlete, because it's not just a one-way street. All young people have people in their lives that impact them.
>
> (Dreher, 2024, para. 9–10)

Coach Staley indicates that while basketball is what she and her athletes do together, athletes' performance on the court is not the end goal. Coach Staley is a coactor alongside her athletes, facilitating exploration of what they are passionate about and seeking to learn how she can provide support.

Similarly, Coach Feldman views being a dream merchant[2] as supporting athletes as whole people, not just athletes. He explains that being a dream merchant involves "carving out what athletes' goals and aspirations are not only with running and the team but also what they're trying to do after their four years in college." Coach Feldman also explained what this looks like in his relationships with athletes.

> I try to walk a fine line of getting to know them as well as possible without it affecting the actual training. What I mean by that is, with a lot of my kids, I know the names of all their immediate family members. I know the degree that they're trying to get. I know the kind of career path they're trying to achieve after they graduate. I usually try to meet with them biweekly, if possible. You know, we have 60 kids on the team. So, sometimes that can be difficult. But I do talk to the kids immediately after all of their races, just to get their feedback.
>
> Aside from that, they need to see that my actions are backed by the words that I'm saying. All these kids are very perceptive. They know somebody that means what they say, and somebody that might just be all talk. I'm of that John Wooden mindset that they don't care how much you know until they know how much you care. So, really emphasizing my interest in their life beyond their [race] times, I think, is so crucial because if they feel that you are invested in them, then there's a trust that really starts to form. I try to treat everybody fairly, but not equally.

Coach Staley and Coach Feldman are both competitive, and they care about their athletes' performance in games and meets. However, they focus on developing trusting relationships with team members as unique individuals first. Doing so allows them to co-create a meaningful experience with athletes in a way that does not center—but also facilitates—positive competitive outcomes.

Co-Creating a Purpose Supports Team Members' Psychological Needs

The athletes in this chapter perceive striving to meet competitive standards as demonstrating leadership. A leader who believes their purpose is guiding the team to winning may pay more attention to the top-performing athletes, which often involves prioritizing their needs. Meanwhile, the rest of the team will remain on the sidelines on the field, the court, and the leaders' priorities. The lower-performing athletes are less likely to improve if they receive fewer resources, including social support and training materials, access to equipment, medical support, or nutrition.

As Self-Determination Theory indicates, athletes' motivation suffers when they do not feel competent or valued by other team members (Deci & Ryan, 1985). So, coaches and athletes in leadership roles focusing on competitive success may initiate divisive practices that reduce their team's capacity for competitive success. In contrast, coactors can cultivate a shared vision of their team's purpose. Rather than prioritizing some team members' athletic performance-based contributions, coactors account for the many valuable ways all team members contribute, as we saw Coach Staley do in Chapter 4, "Share the Power." In this way, team members express power with each other.

Inviting athletes to determine their shared purpose motivates them to be engaged members of their team and enables everyone to contribute their power within. Team members can share their ideas, identify overlaps, and work through conflicting perspectives on what the team should prioritize. Athletes may have their own reasons for being part of the team. However, establishing a shared purpose provides direction for everyone. By establishing a foundation constructed of their shared purpose, the team members have a foundation that clarifies why they are working together.

Leadership Constrains Purpose

The traditional hierarchical definition of leadership often results in recognizing one person as a leader (Wakefield, 2017). College athletic teams typically have one captain, or a few at most. This leadership model can cultivate the belief that athletes must compete with their teammates to achieve a position at the top of the hierarchy and become a captain. Athletes who are not selected as leaders learn that they are supposed to follow their coach's instructions and the captains' example. So, athletes who understand their purpose differently can feel they must prove they deserve to be a captain; this feeling can result in prioritizing the coach's vision and avoiding voicing their perspective. As a result, the team leadership structure becomes regulatory. Athletes in a regulatory structure are unlikely to offer alternative views and do not learn how to work collaboratively.

However, as a coach, you can express power with athletes from the beginning of the season by inviting team members to define their purpose. You can emphasize that when all team members are coactors, athletes do not have to prove they fit pre-determined leadership criteria. They define why they are there, what they need from one another, and how they will support each other.

Collegiate coaches often expect team captains to manage team logistics, communicate with the coach and other student-athletes, model desired behaviors, represent their team to the public, and manage relationships among team members (Brgoch et al., 2020). These expectations indicate that coaches expect an athlete leader to fulfill a limited set of responsibilities—they are primarily expected to follow and uphold guidelines set by the coach. If you want athletes to share their purpose, you must also encourage them to consider their contributions to the team beyond the logistical tasks associated with training and competing.

Athlete leaders are also often expected to manage intra-team relationships by providing motivation and inspiration and building relationships among teammates (Brgoch et al., 2020). Athletes who participated in my research explained that a leader's purpose is to support their team members. This support included pursuing athletic goals and creating a positive atmosphere that supports team members' enjoyment of the sport. To do this effectively, the coach must also contribute by modeling behaviors and creating a supportive atmosphere.

While athletes have peer relationships that are different from their coach-athlete relationships, Polyvagal Theory reminds us that we need to feel safe to connect with others. Athlete relationships do not operate in a sphere unaffected by their coach, or a tier beneath the coach-athlete dynamic, as a hierarchical structure may encourage us to envision. On a coactive team, coaches and athletes acknowledge their interconnectedness and act accordingly; they are threads in the same braid. If athletes feel fully supported and see that their coach is invested in a shared purpose, they will be more capable of supporting one another. If they do not feel safe, they are more likely to engage in self-preservation, limiting their capacity for engaging with others supportively. To create a team with intentional, supportive relationships, coaches must be coactors alongside athletes, rather than leaders positioned above them. Similarly, coaches must create a team structure that enables athletes to be coactors alongside one another rather than designating a select few as leaders.

If supporting one another leads to effective collaboration, co-defining the team's purpose according to what athletes want to experience together is a foundational step to a collaborative team. Previous research suggests that when coaches and athlete leaders engage in supportive, relationship-oriented behaviors, team members have greater intrinsic motivation to learn, challenge themselves, and pursue team goals. They have enhanced confidence in their team's ability to achieve goals and greater enjoyment of the sport (Price & Weiss, 2013). As an additional outcome, co-defining the team's purpose and focusing on the experience team members want to share may lead to greater competitive success.

Steps to Co-Create Purpose

- Reframe the "purpose" of participating in sport. As discussed throughout this chapter, a coach must open the door for athletes to propose a purpose other than winning competitions.

  As a team, reflect on and discuss the benefits of participating in sport. Invite team members to share the positives they experience. Together, assess how many benefits were named that were not based on winning competitions.

  Next, consider how the other benefits can enhance experiences and, as a result, set team members up to perform at their best athletically.

  Finally, discuss how your team members' everyday actions influence which benefits they tend to focus on. Reflect on and share if and how focusing on these benefits creates an environment that supports development and enjoyment.
- Collaboratively establish a team purpose. Engage in a dialogue to explore what the athletes view as the purpose of their involvement with the team. Encourage them to reflect on their reasons for joining and contributing to team efforts.

  Remember that athletes may feel like they must be competition-oriented and hesitate to share a purpose other than winning competitions. To encourage athletes to share other ideas, reflect on your reasons for coaching the team and share them. As a coach, you may be assessed by your win-loss record. Put this metric aside. Share what motivates you to build your team and show up to practice every day. Then, invite team members to share what motivates them to engage. Compare and discuss similarities and differences among motivations.

  Using a consensus-building process, identify a shared purpose that will remind everyone why they are on this team. The team can post their purpose in a visible place, like on the wall of their locker room or bracelets that they wear. Reminders help athletes keep their purpose in mind.

- Address challenges. Your team's purpose is unique. Some arise because you have all come together to create a community and pursue a purpose unavailable elsewhere. Consequently, the team's purpose may conflict with the priorities of the organization and the culture within which your team exists.

  It is valuable to consider how athletes could respond when facing challenges to their purpose. For example, imagine another team within your department practices twice a day, at 5 a.m. and 4 p.m., with the mindset that more time training is the key to winning. Meanwhile, your team may establish the expectation that athletes cannot reap all the benefits of their training without recovery. So, your team may create a mantra, like, "Rest is equally important as hard training."

  If members of other teams criticize your athletes for not training as often, they can come back to this phrase as a reminder of why the team trains as it does; their training is designed based on their mutually determined commitment to prioritize recovery. With a clearly defined team purpose, athletes can explain this to other teams as well. As a team, you schedule training sessions guided by your purpose. Your team's purpose is unique, so your team does not need to operate in the same way as others. Athletes can define their purpose according to the experience their team members want to have together.

Reflection Questions

- What is your purpose for coaching?
- What do you want athletes on your team to experience at practice? What do you want them to experience when they compete?
- How might your purpose influence the athletes you coach to perceive their purpose on your team? Are there adjustments you want to make to help athletes feel recognized and valued as whole people?
- Do you invite athletes to help you define your team's purpose each season? If so, how can you maximize the involvement of all team members to account for their perspectives? If not, how might you start involving athletes in defining the team's purpose?
- How do you define growth? What might it look like for your team to pause and process together, to determine what they need and want from their experience?

Notes

1 This is the 2024–2025 Smith College Tennis Team's purpose, which they developed collectively.
2 Coach Feldman attributes his use of the term "dream merchant" to the album Dream Merchant Vol 1. produced by 9th Wonder.

References

Batliwala, S. (2011). *Feminist leadership for social transformation: Clearing the conceptual cloud*. Crea.

Brgoch, S. M., Lower-Hoppe, L. M., Newman, T. J., Hutton, T. A. (2020). Exploring team captain roles associated with athlete leadership classifications: Perspectives from collegiate coaches. *Journal of Sport Behavior*, *43*(1), 28–49.

Deci, E. L., & Ryan, R. M. (1985). *Intrinsic motivation and self-determination in human behavior*. Plenum Press.

Denison, J., & Mills, J. P. (2014). Planning for distance running: Coaching with Foucault. *Sports Coaching Review*, *3*(1), 1–16. https://doi.org/10.1080/21640629.2014.953005

Denison, J., Mills, J. P., & Konoval, T. (2017). Sports' disciplinary legacy and the challenge of 'coaching differently'. *Sport, Education and Society*, *22*(6), 772–783. https://doi.org/10.1080/13573322.2015.1061986

Dreher, L. (2024, May 30). *The excellence of Dawn Staley: South Carolina head coach talks championship, being a 'dream merchant' and growth of women's hoops*. Slam. www.slamonline.com/the-magazine/250/dawn-staley-south-carolina-cover-story/

Durkheim, É. (1912/1915). *The elementary forms of religious life* (J. D. Swan transl.). Georges Allen & Unwin. (Original work published 1912.)

Pape, M. (2019). Gender segregation and trajectories of organizational change: The underrepresentation of women in sports leadership. *Gender & Society*, *34*(1), 81–105. https://doi.org/10.1177/0891243219867914

Pizarro J. J., Zumeta, L. N, Bouchat, P., Włodarczyk, A., Rimé, B., Basabe, N., Amutio, A., & Páez, D. (2022). Emotional processes, collective behavior, and social movements: A meta-analytic review of collective effervescence outcomes during collective gatherings and demonstrations. *Frontiers in Psychology*, *13*, 1–28. https://doi.org/10.3389/fpsyg.2022.974683

Price, M. S., & Weiss, M. R. (2013). Relationships among coach leadership, peer leadership, and adolescent athletes' psychosocial and team outcomes: A test of transformational leadership theory. *Journal of Applied Sport Psychology*, *25*(2), 265–279. http://dx.doi.org/10.1080/10413200.2012.725703

Suyemoto, K. L., & Ballou, M. B. (2007). Conducted monotones to coacted harmonies: A feminist (re)conceptualization of leadership addressing race, class, and gender. In J. L. Chin, B. Lott, J. K. Rice, & J. Sanchez-Hucles (Eds.), *Women and leadership: Transforming visions and diverse voices* (pp. 35–54). Blackwell Publishing.

VeneKlasen, L., & Miller, V. (2007). *A new weave of power, people & politics: The action guide for advocacy and citizen participation*. Stylus Publishing.

Wakefield, S. (2017). Transformative and feminist leadership for women's rights. Oxfam America Research Backgrounder Series. www.oxfamamerica.org/explore/research-publications/transformative-feminist-leadership-womens-rights/

6 Building a Foundation through Alignment, Not Sameness

Team members must clearly define the team's purpose to determine how they'll achieve it. Recognizing and valuing differences among team members is foundational for engaging in equitable practices that enable them to achieve their shared purpose (Batltiwala, 2011). This process can begin with discussing personal values and principles. Teammates can learn what everyone's values mean to them and why they matter.

Our values inform what we need from others to feel supported, as well as how we strive to support others. Principles are the guidelines we use to make decisions about our actions (Vealey & Chase, 2016). As stated in Chapter 1, Why We Need to Think Differently about Athlete Leadership Development, it is unrealistic to expect all team members to share the same values and principles. However, team members may find alignment among them; our values and principles may be different, but we may find that our desired outcomes of enacting them are similar.

For example, one team member may value home while another may value trust. They might want different types of support, but both may be committed to developing strong, caring relationships as an outcome of putting their values into action. As team members learn about one another's values, they can develop shared principles or expectations, for how they will engage with one another. In doing so, no team member is required to change what is important to them, or what they need from others. Rather, team members develop a shared understanding of what informs each person's inclinations and behaviors, while also considering the potential impact of their own inclinations and behaviors on others.

DOI: 10.4324/9781003605485-6

As John Amaechi (2021) states, "People make choices. And those choices make culture" (p. 149). Team discussions about values and principles enable athletes to be intentional about their actions, thereby intentionally building the culture they want to have. As demonstrated in the athletes' dialogue in this chapter, values and principles come to life through everyday practices.

Coming Together across Differences

Sport teams often have a set of values that guide their work. As Piper explained:

> We have our team core values that we're all bought into because that's the culture that people have committed to, and everyone chose Midwestern University. That's a buy-in right there. You had other options, you had other places you could go, you had different sports you can play, but you ended up here. So, you've bought into this program. So, now the next thing is making sure we're all on the same page and giving people voices.
>
> Something I did to cultivate buy-in is I made a Google form with the team about what our priorities were. Part of the reason I really wanted to do that was that I needed people to understand they had a say. I gave questions, everyone filled out the questions, and we shared them. It was interesting because I answered all my questions and I was like, "I think these are it, these are great answers. I really think this is what it is for our team." We voted and some of them were there, but some of them weren't, because the rest of the team was like, "No, this is really important to us."
>
> So, I think for creating buy-in, I was like, "If that's what's important to our team, that's what's important to our team." Just because that wasn't my first answer as a leader, it doesn't mean that's not what's most important for our team. So, I think part of creating buy-in is making sure people have a say, and they need to understand that their opinion and their voice matter. It doesn't mean anything I say or want is what goes, and the same for them, but they need to know that they have a space and that they're valued in coming forward with their opinion, and that it's important to the team. I think it's really easy to buy into something like that, and you have to believe in it.

As Piper indicated, coaches recruit college athletes, who sometimes choose a team based on the coaches' and team members' stated values. However, we cannot assume everyone has an equal investment in these values or that all team members interpret values in the same way. The team's guiding principles and values depend on which perspectives are accounted for when establishing expectations. As a formal leader, Piper was striving to be inclusive. She recognized that not everyone would share her values and tried to account for that through voting. However, as discussed in Chapter 2, "The New Framework: The Coactive Process," majority votes prioritize commonalities among the many rather than addressing potential impact on all team members.

Is it necessary for the team to have a shared set of values to prioritize? Who does declared "team values" serve if the values identified are not actually all team members' top values?

Conformity to expected team values and principles does not ensure athletes' investment in or comfort with them. If a team member feels pressured to accept a team value they don't share, they are unlikely to prioritize demonstrating that value through their actions. Furthermore, if the value conflicts with their own, this will likely thwart their sense of relatedness with team members. Feeling undervalued or not accounted for may lead to disengagement or dropout.

Even sharing the same value does not ensure team members have the same needs or commitments. Athletes indicate that although team members can share a value, they might define it differently. The following dialogue among athletes conveys their different perspectives on values, including diversity and respect:

Molly: Putting yourself in other peoples' shoes is a big thing because everyone comes from different walks of life. It's hard to put yourself in that position when you've never experienced it, but I think that's important to try to do and realize that not everyone's like you.

Ana: I'd say I'm very diverse and accepting because I do come from a background of two different races. My mom is white, my dad's Black, so growing up, I think that was a really big aspect of my life, even if sometimes I didn't really understand certain things. I think growing up with that has helped me be more accepting of others and others' views. I think that's helped me be a leader on my team just because we do have a lot of different people from different backgrounds, and I think that really is a big portion of coming together as one.

Mina: I have a friend who's very religious, and I have a friend who doesn't believe in anything. We're still teammates, we still work together, but they have an understanding that, "Ok, that's what you believe, that's what you don't believe, that's totally fine. I'm not gonna look at you any different." That's just what we do. To me, it was very cool to see people come together even though they don't have the same beliefs or wants in their life. It was cool that there was understanding. Then I ask questions. I asked my friend so many questions about her religion because we're totally different. Then I asked my other friend questions, and she gave her reasons, and they were all valid reasons. So, it was just cool that we could all come together and ask questions and not be like rude or get upset about it. It also was like, "Ok, now I understand how to ask questions." Maybe they told me, "That's not ok, or that is ok." It was cool to be comfortable asking those questions and being comfortable giving the response.

Jackie: I think a lot of people judge other people by what they see on the outside and not what they see on the inside. Sometimes people are like, "That person's just doing that because they can," but sometimes, when you sit down and talk to someone, you actually get to know them and understand why they are the way that they are. It's easier to work with them when you're able to sit down and talk to people rather than just being like, "That's how you are? I don't want to deal with you." That's how I perceive myself as a leader, I don't want to judge people because of what I've seen or what I've heard, I want to be able to sit down and talk to them and get to know them.

Lilah: Every practice, we put our hands in the middle and do a break, and we do it multiple times a meet. It just brings people on teams and leaders and even coaches together, and then you feel more of a whole being, all together in one small space. [I saw] an image… of many people's hands in the middle, and the hands were all different colors, like a rainbow. I think that image is important because, I don't want to bring race into it, but I was raised in a very open family. I'm very open to people whether you're white, brown, black, purple, green, it's all the same.

Kai: Leaders have respect for others, even though they're at the top of the organizations. My coach shows respect to everyone on our team and treats them like they're equal. She praises players a lot when they do something good, doesn't deny [the] player's personality, and shows love by words and actions like a hug, a text message, or having casual and private conversations with players.

Kenza: People respond, and even I respond more to captains and leaders who are respectful and treat everyone the same.

Fiona: The main thing that I have an issue with when thinking of our captains, and I know that other people on the team have issues with too, is the way that one particular captain chooses to treat other people. She sees herself as a leader, and she has this captain position, but she uses it to look down on other people rather than lead them. The tone that we get from her is kind of condescending, and the way that she communicates makes other people feel like they're in the wrong and they shouldn't even try. Our other captain communicates in a way that's ideal and shows respect. When it comes to communicating, she takes what other people are going through into account and realizes that before she addresses someone about an issue that they're having or that she has with the way that they're doing something. It comes off as a lot more respectful because she puts a lot more thought into the way that she says it and the things that she says.

Each person's values and principles are shaped by who they are. As Batliwala (2011) explains, the self is a critical component of how a person defines leadership; people cannot separate themselves from their identities and experiences. The athletes' dialogue demonstrates that experiences inform their values and principles and that they aim to demonstrate them through their actions. For example, Fiona indicated the importance of demonstrating respect—and how respect is and is not demonstrated—by comparing the actions of two team captains. As discussed above, in addition to naming their values and principles, the team members must discuss how they will show them through their everyday practices.

Connecting Values to Shared Practices

Rather than assigning a set of shared values, discussing personal values and principles shows team members that they do not have to be the same to be impactful. Rather, as Mina discussed above, differences create an opportunity for athletes to learn from one another and stretch their perspectives. Team members can practice engaging with openness and curiosity, asking questions and attentively listening to better understand. The athletes who participated in the dialogue indicated that they learn from their teammates. Several discussed approaching people different from themselves with curiosity, inviting an exchange of perspectives. Athletes can also practice setting and respecting boundaries, such as when a team member does not feel comfortable answering a question. Mina acknowledged that she does not need to share the same viewpoint as her teammates to treat them respectfully.

However, coaction goes beyond the foundational act of respecting others. Respect does not ensure active support. Curiosity about team members' values opens the door to learning how to support team members in the way that they need, not how we assume they want to be treated.

Claiming diversity as a value can also lead to collaboration and inclusion, but this is not guaranteed. It also may lead to conformity and exclusion, depending on whose explanation is prioritized. For example, Lilah indicated that ignoring differences and focusing on similarities demonstrates valuing diversity. Similarly, Kai and Kenza said every team member should be treated the same. Given this understanding of diversity, athletes might avoid asking questions that require them to confront differences. Every person has different needs; if athletes or coaches fail to acknowledge those differences, they will struggle to support each other. Aiming to demonstrate that valuing diversity in the two ways the athletes discussed would lead to vastly different outcomes.

A white athlete, who may not have reflected on her racial identity's impact on her everyday experiences, proposed not acknowledging differences. This is something many white people are socialized to do (Abaied & Perry, 2021). Her privileged position enabled her to view race as irrelevant, whereas her teammates of color cannot ignore race because of systemic discrimination. Athletes of color consistently confront bias through experiences like being the target of a racial slur or observing discrimination in their social surroundings. Among NCAA college head coaches, less than 20% identify as Black, Indigenous, and People of Color (BIPOC).[1] White athletes frequently see people who look like them in formal leadership roles. In contrast, BIPOC athletes have significantly fewer opportunities to be coached by someone with their racial identity. It's challenging to imagine obtaining a formal leadership role if you have not seen someone like you represented in that role.

You also cannot assume that a value benefits everyone if you define it without paying attention to its associated behaviors. Research shows that treating even seemingly positive organizational practices as unbiased can perpetuate exclusion (Knoppers & Anthonissen, 2001; Shaw & Frisby, 2006). For example, college athletes are taught to prioritize unity because team members must work together to be competitively successful. However, athletes face contradictory instructions about achieving unity. Although some frame acceptance as uniting as one team, saying that differences don't matter erases individuality. If we don't acknowledge diverse identities and experiences, athletes cannot voice varied perspectives. Instead, we end up encouraging one leader to employ power over others rather than express power with one another.

Notably, several athletes discussed learning to recognize and value differences through lived experiences like judgment. This understanding of diversity demonstrates the relationship between the self and a person's expectations of how team members work together. If valuing diversity is defined as seeking to understand others who are different, team members can recognize each other's identities. Valuing difference enables all athletes to contribute in their own way, informed by who they are, in collaboration with others.

The athletes' discussion of respect indicated that they are invested in putting values into action with teammates and coaches who demonstrate these values. For example, athletes described respect based on how their coaches and teammates treated them and how this treatment made them feel. Coaches' and teammates' relationship-oriented behaviors, like taking their perspectives into account, offering praise, and investing time and attention in one-on-one conversations, make team members feel valued and enable them to work well together. In contrast, treating everyone the same does not result in equal outcomes, because not everyone needs or wants the same things. There will be times when an athlete needs more one-on-one time for skill instruction or emotional support. Some athletes prefer feedback in the moment; others want to schedule a meeting outside of practice. By engaging in equitable rather than identical practices, providing the type of support each team member needs, all team members can feel equally valuable.

If athletes have a clear understanding of their shared purpose, what matters is that they work together effectively to achieve that purpose. Discussing values and principles is a foundational step at the beginning of each season, so that team members can best support one another. Different values and principles may lead people to the same purpose. This means that team members' values and principles *align*, not that they are the same.

Identifying Shared Practices to Achieve the Team's Purpose

As discussed in the opening of this chapter, our values inform what we need to feel seen and supported by others, as well as how we strive to support others. Yoga instructor Nikki and yoga instructor and personal trainer KC explained their values and how their values inform their actions. This combination helps them achieve their purpose as co-owners of a yoga studio and gym.

Nikki: [My values are] home and freedom.

KC: My values are freedom and order.

Nikki: It's hard for me… to really differentiate who I am as a person versus who I am at work… My work is just really embedded into my life… I've always gotten along with people, I'm friendly, but I never felt a really strong sense of community anywhere. So that was an important aspect of the yoga studio for me, wanting to create an environment where people felt at home and where they felt like they belonged and they felt like they fit in. [It is] an open space to be yourself and be celebratory of everyone's different life experience. By and large, that has happened… within the community. People have got to know each other a lot and created little sub-communities that are a part of the overarching role.

Freedom is important always to both of us. [For example,] the freedom to make our own schedule… We can make decisions, and if we want to do something different we don't have to ask anybody, we just decide to do it.

So, I think that giving other people freedom in turn is an important part of that and it ties into our philosophy of how… it's very rare for us to step in and give any sort of notes on what [our teachers are] doing or how they're teaching because we just want them to be able to have the experience of evolving on their own and supporting them as they continue to evolve, because if it's important to me, it might be important to you, too. We don't want to have this really strong hierarchical system within the yoga studio.

KC: At a distance almost seems like [my values, freedom and order, are] contradictory but they're not. Making our own schedule and creating gives us both a sense of freedom in our lives. So, that spills into how we're operating our businesses. And then order is one of my values. So, when it comes to policy or strategy, because… it kind of sounds like things are hanging pretty loose and we want that, but my college degree is in business and organizational communications, my dad owned a gym, and my mom has been an administrator for a very long time, so I'm coming from a lot of ordered thinking. So, I have kind of had to be the one to be like, "We should really put structure here."

Nikki: That's probably my greatest weakness. Imposing order on people is very, very difficult for me. It makes me feel really, really uncomfortable, even though I know intellectually people crave orderly environments. I believe that with my whole heart. I know somebody has to do it. I just do not want it to be me. And I also see the benefit of it if done in a way that still gives people freedom. I want there to be order so that there's certainty where we can have it… You know, if we have a way of doing things, you can explain how to do it and then they can learn how to do it and just have it.

Since implementing structure lies within KC's strengths, KC handles those activities. Likewise, Nikki can engage in actions that play into her strengths. The key is alignment. Nikki believes structure supports the experience they want to create for members of their yoga studio and gym, even though order is not a top value for her. KC and Nikki share the value of freedom, and their explanation of freedom demonstrates their own needs. For example, they appreciate the ability to determine their own schedules. Their values also inform how they aim to support others, such as allowing their employees to teach in a way that feels right to them.

In a similar vein, Coach Johnson-Crowder did not emphasize the values team members need to have, but how she expects team members to interact with one another to co-create a positive team experience. Athletes learn how to care for themselves and one another through their experiences on Coach Johnson-Crowder's team. In doing so, they may also achieve several of the behavioral outcomes that are valued in sport, such as working hard, but these arise from experiencing a culture of mutual support. Coach Johnson-Crowder explained,

> The determination, the work ethic, yes, we discuss it when needed, but it's not something that I'm like, "Here are the core values: determination…" It doesn't really work like that for me. But what I do drill when it comes to the values is how we treat each other in this space. So, I am huge on we don't do mean girl behavior… because… on a mental health side, it says so much about how these kids have taught themselves to cope. There are so many of them who have no idea what true self-acceptance looks like. So, they're constantly picking at other people around them for being different or moving differently. Then, when I call them out on that, I don't do it in a way where it's like, "Hey, you, Sarah!" I'll have a team meeting, and I'll speak broadly about the concept, because again, I don't want it to be pointing fingers. But what I do need is everyone to know, this is for everybody. So, if you cannot support a safe space, I completely understand if you do not want to be in it anymore. Period.
>
> If you cannot express your thoughts and feelings in a way where you're not causing harm, this probably isn't the room for you. Now, if you struggle with that, but you're willing to work towards that honestly and openly, oh, come on. Cause I'm all for the healing. But the biggest thing that I push when it comes to team tenets, compassion, honesty, and visibility, would be the best way to put it 'cause everything falls underneath that. If I'm asking you to work hard, I also have to be compassionate and understanding when you don't have it. If you just don't have it today, and I have to adjust the workout, I'm not gonna adjust it with the shame lens of, "Oh, you guys are tired. Alright, I guess we're cutting this off." No, it's like, "Okay, y'all are kinda beat up today, we're gonna dial it back

> to this. It doesn't really look like your bodies are responding too well." So, I feel like by living in the team through those tenets and then having them be the core piece bringing us all together. It allows us now to actually exist in the "determination" and the "set a goal, go after it," "respect others." How do you teach somebody to respect others when they don't respect themselves? How do I ask you to respect someone else's boundaries when your boundaries have been trampled on your entire life? It doesn't work. So, I try my hardest to hit the core of what I think will impact the team and then allow the other pieces to be the reinforcing factors.

No one adopts values on command. Remember the threads in the braid of coaction: self. Team members bring their full selves, including past experiences, to the team. The way they expect to be treated and how they treat others are informed by all their prior relationships, experiences, and values. As Coach Johnson-Crowder points out, if team members have not experienced supportive, respectful, collaborative relationships, how can they show up in this way? By prioritizing the experience she wants athletes to have, Coach Johnson-Crowder determines how she wants to interact with them, exemplifying expressing power with them. This informs how athletes interact with her and one another, and they are more capable of engaging in actions that support their athletic performance.

As Coach Feldman discussed in Chapter 3, "Cultivating Coaction through Valuing Team Members as Their Full Selves," we must accompany our words with action to build trust. Coach Feldman also discussed his intent to create a particular team experience.

> We define success on our team as "doing the best you can with what you got where you're at." And if people are doing the bare minimum or just being compliant, I have to broach the subject that, you know, why are we here? And then that usually leads to a conversation that is shedding light on something that I didn't know about, or they didn't know how to express. But that's kind of how the cycle works.

Similar to Coach Johnson-Crowder, Coach Feldman seeks to support each team member so they can be invested and engaged. As the athletes discussed earlier in this chapter, both coaches approach athletes with curiosity and a desire to understand their needs. As Nikki and KC indicated, this enables team members to work together effectively.

Steps to Discuss Values and Principles and Identify Practices

1 Team members must feel like they can openly express their own values and principles without fear of criticism. Clearly state that it is expected and beneficial for team members to have different values and principles. This is an opportunity for team members to practice perspective-taking[2] and consider what informs their teammates', and their own, values and principles.

Two activities can help you start creating an inclusive and supportive environment, but be aware that doing so takes time. These activities are a starting point, but the team must continuously invest in applying what they learn to maintain trust.

The first activity is writing personal permission slips (Brown, 2021). The second is setting ground rules.

Writing personal permission slips requires team members to be introspective. Ask them to consider what personal challenges might prevent them from openly expressing themselves. For example, an athlete may be hesitant to speak up because they may not have had many opportunities to do so. So, they may write a permission slip to commit to sharing their perspective even though it may feel unfamiliar or uncomfortable. Another athlete may have concerns that seem within their control, such as, "I'm afraid that teammates will disagree with me." However, such a fear may stem from previous situations when teammates made a decision without accounting for their perspective. An athlete with this concern can also write a permission slip for expressing themselves. Overcoming this concern involves both individual and relational challenges, but permission slips for both athletes serve as a reminder for the individual that they have power within and they are encouraged to share their concerns with team members. This opens the door to teammates expressing power with one another as they create ground rules for how they will support one another.

Ground rules address concerns about the social environment by establishing expectations for working together. A ground rule that could be paired with the permission slip written by the first athlete above could be "Share the floor." This ground rule encourages team members to encourage their team members to contribute to discussions. A ground rule that could be paired with the permission slip written by the second athlete mentioned above might be, "You can disagree with a statement but not a person." This ground rule encourages team members to see disagreement as acceptable, because people have different perspectives. However, it also reminds everyone that no one is defined by one thing they said. Teammates should not disrespect each other due to a disagreement. Instead, they can try to understand what the person meant and why they made the statement. This may stretch teammates' perspectives and encourage them to reflect on their own beliefs. Teammates might still disagree, but they will understand one another better. Ground rules serve as a reminder to team members that they are not all the same; they cannot assume that others want to be treated in the way that they want to be treated. Rather, to express power with one another as they work toward their shared purpose, they must learn from teammates about their different needs and intentionally act in ways that support one another.

2 Ask each team member to write down two to three of their core values, along with an explanation of what each value means to them. Once team members have had time to reflect, invite everyone to write their values on a shared discussion board, such as a whiteboard or digital forum. Discuss team members' definition of their values. Explore where there is alignment in definitions, as well as how differences expand the athletes' perspectives. When conflicting examples arise, discuss the outcomes to consider how team members would be impacted. Before moving to the next step, ask the athletes what they have learned about, or from, one another.
3 Ask each team member to reflect on how the core values they named inform their everyday practices. How do they strive to interact with other people to stay aligned with their values? Invite team members to write down these practices on the shared discussion board.
4 Ask each team member to reflect on how their core values inform what they need to feel supported. What do they expect from others, based on their own values?
5 Invite all team members to review the practices they engage in. Then, review the practices their teammates need and expect from others.

6 As a team, discuss what you all observe. Are there ways you might alter the practices teammates tend to engage in? Are there ways athletes want to be supported that fit well within someone's tendencies or skill set? How do the practices listed contribute (or not) to achieving your team's purpose?
7 Invite each team member to name two practices they will commit to engaging in that feel right to them based on their own needs and strengths, and that are supportive of others' needs. Remember, as coactors, all athletes contribute in different, equally important ways to achieving the team's purpose. Team members' unique inclinations and abilities are assets.
8 Review how team members need to be supported. Is anything missing from the practices team members committed to? If so, discuss how team members can develop new skills as they strive to support one another.

The process of sharing values and identifying practices is dynamic. The practices that team members commit to are a starting point for intentional engagement and having shared expectations, or principles, for how they will interact with one another. They are not the only ways athletes will support each other. As discussed earlier in this chapter, team members' values and principles are informed by their experiences and may shift over time. As team members interact, the ways they want to support one another and be supported may change. Take time throughout the season to check in. Are the practices received by team members as intended? Are any changes needed to work together more effectively? The coactive process is ongoing.

Reflection

1 What are your core values? How do you put those values into practice in your interactions with team members? How do your values inform what you need to be supported?
2 Are all team members equipped with skills and experience to support one another in the ways you expect them to? How do you model supportive behaviors and seek to learn about challenges team members may face in effectively supporting others?
3 How does your team make decisions? Whose perspectives are prioritized? How is the impact of decisions on team members accounted for?

4 Does your team discuss specific practices that will help you all achieve your shared purpose? Are team members expected to contribute identically? Do team members have the opportunity to share the ways that they would most like to contribute?

Notes

1 This statistic comes from the NCAA Demographics Database published in 2024, which offers limited options for head coaches to self-identify. Based on the categories provided for race/ethnicity, 11% identify as Black, 3% identify as Hispanic/Latino, 1% identify as two or more races, 1% identify as international (assumed to not identify as white, because this category is distinct from white), 1% identify as Asian, 1% have unknown racial/ethnic identities, and less than 1% identify as American Indian/Alaska Native or Native Hawaiian/Pacific Islander. For more information, visit https://www.ncaa.org/sports/2018/12/13/ncaa-demographics-database.aspx

2 For an explanation of perspective-taking, watch Perspective Taking created by RISE: www.youtube.com/watch?v=tqz7UcCgbLA. For recommendations about engaging your athletes in perspective-taking, read Perspective Taking Is Essential for Student Development, Learning by Courtney A. Gay: https://risetowin.org/perspectives/2017/8-28/perspective-taking-is-essential-for-student-development-learning/index.html

References

Abaied, J. L. & Perry, S. P. (2021). Socialization of racial ideology by White parents. *Cultural Diversity & Ethnic Minority Psychology*, *27*, 431–440. https://doi.org/10.1037/cdp0000454

Amaechi, J. (2021). *The promises of giants*. Nicholas Brealey Publishing.

Batliwala, S. (2011). *Feminist leadership for social transformation: Clearing the conceptual cloud*. Crea.

Brown, B. (2021). *Dare to lead: Read-along workbook*. Brené Brown. https://brenebrown.com/resources/dare-to-lead-read-along-workbook/

Knoppers, A., & Anthonissen, A. (2001). Meanings given to performance in Dutch sport organizations: Gender and racial/ethnic subtexts. *Sociology of Sport Journal*, *18*(3), 302–316. https://doi.org/10.1123/ssj.18.3.302

Shaw, S., & Frisby, W. (2006). Can Gender Equity Be More Equitable?: Promoting an Alternative Frame for Sport Management Research, Education, and Practice. *Journal of Sport Management*, *20*(4), 483–509. https://doi.org/10.1123/jsm.20.4.483

Vealey, R. S., & Chase, M. A. (2016). *Best practice for youth sport*. Human Kinetics.

Conclusion

Your Team's Coactive Process

As a coach, you can encourage athletes to share responsibilities and view themselves as leaders, but the traditional hierarchical leadership structure makes it harder for team members to become active contributors. By appointing team captains or designating the most senior athletes as team leaders, we perpetuate an exclusionary leadership structure. Enabling athletes to recognize their ability to contribute to the team and think critically requires us to think and act beyond what is typically done.

An athlete cannot fully realize their strengths if they are treated as a follower who must be molded into a leader. If someone strives to be recognized as a leader within a traditional sport hierarchy, we may neglect how their unique strengths, skills, and qualities could contribute to the team's success. An athlete's understanding of their own strengths may narrow. Team members who are "developed" as leaders are likely to contribute in similar ways, limiting the team's collective capacity and their ability to support one another effectively. Additionally, when the molding concludes, the new leaders may possess new abilities or knowledge, but they will be accustomed to following.

Instead of replicating these patterns, we can consider what *could* be done to meet athletes' current needs. As Denison and Mills (2014) said, "A coach needs to think beyond 'changing the athlete,' e.g., [their] perception of control, and instead develop new practices that disrupt how athletes are positioned by continually being seen as the target of their coaches' interventions" (p. 8). Athletes are already valuable, capable, contributors with unique assets to offer to their team. What if we sought to hone and expand each athlete's strengths within

DOI: 10.4324/9781003605485-7

the context of the team? Remember, team members who feel competent, feel like they have autonomy, and who feel valued and connected are more likely to be intrinsically motivated to actively contribute to team efforts (Deci & Ryan, 1985). Feeling seen and supported also facilitates learning and collaboration (Porges, 1995, 2022).

As you have learned throughout this book, moving away from the traditional understanding of leadership as a status to be earned and shifting to cultivating coactive teams supports the involvement and growth of all team members. VeneKlasen and Miller's (2007) framework for thinking about power, discussed in Chapter 2, "The New Framework: The Coactive Process," encourages us to consider how we use our power and how we create or limit opportunities for others to use their power.

As coaches, if we strive to express power with the athletes on our team, we should not expect them to seek titles, ranks, or roles. Instead, we can invest in discussions about the experience they want to have and how they can all actively contribute to co-creating that experience. These discussions open the door to practices that cultivate all team members' growth as intentional and impactful coactors and their perceptions of each other as valuable and capable coactors.

When team members are valued for the unique qualities they bring to the team, they can express their full selves rather than try to meet others' imposed expectations. Team members can draw upon various strengths and develop strategies that incorporate and maximize everyone's capabilities. In doing so, athletes are more likely to enjoy learning together, athletically and personally. Winning competitions becomes one aspect of their successful collaboration and care for one another, rather than the sole determinant of success. Team members redefine success as they engage in the coactive process together.

As you and your team use this book to work through your coactive process, fill in the blanks in the following outline. Remember that engaging in coaction is not a linear or one-time process. Your team will likely revisit different stages throughout the season. Repeat the entire coactive process with each new season and each new team.

Together, we can each use the power that we have to flip the narrative from tired, deficit-based leadership development strategies to inclusive, asset-based strategies to facilitate collaboration among our team members and enable each team member to thrive. We can all be coactors.

Outline for Cultivating Your Coactive Team

The experience that our team members want to have when they are together is:

____

____

____

We have come together as a team for this purpose.

Our team's ground rules are:

____

____

____

We each bring experiences, perspectives, and strengths to the team. With this in mind, we are all committed to finding ways to apply our strengths and support our teammates' ability to do the same. Below is a list of at least one practice each team member will engage in to intentionally contribute their strengths alongside others in a way that helps us achieve our purpose.

Team member's name: ______________________________

Team member's chosen practice:

____

(continue list to include every team member)

References

Deci, E. L., & Ryan, R. M. (1985). *Intrinsic motivation and self-determination in human behavior*. Plenum Press.

Denison, J., & Mills, J. P. (2014). Planning for distance running: Coaching with Foucault. *Sports Coaching Review*, *3*(1), 1–16. https://doi.org/10.1080/21640629.2014.953005

Porges, S. W. (1995). Orienting in a defensive world: Mammalian modifications of our evolutionary heritage. A Polyvagal Theory. *Psychophysiology, 32*(4), 301–18. https://doi.org/10.1111/j.1469-8986.1995.tb01213.x

Porges S. W. (2022). Polyvagal Theory: A science of safety. *Frontiers in Integrative Neuroscience*, *16*, 1–15. https://doi.org/10.3389/fnint.2022.871227

VeneKlasen, L., & Miller, V. (2007). *A new weave of power, people & politics: The action guide for advocacy and citizen participation*. Stylus Publishing.

Index

For Product Safety Concerns and Information please contact our EU
representative GPSR@taylorandfrancis.com Taylor & Francis Verlag GmbH,
Kaufingerstraße 24, 80331 München, Germany

Printed and bound by CPI Group (UK) Ltd, Croydon, CR0 4YY
14/09/2026
02216243-0013